NORTH KOREA – PARIAH?

NORTH KOREA – PARIAH?

D. ELLSWORTH BLANC (EDITOR)

Novinka Books
Huntington, NY

Senior Editors: Susan Boriotti and Donna Dennis
Editorial Coordinator: Tatiana Shohov
Office Manager: Annette Hellinger
Graphics: Wanda Serrano
Book Production: Matthew Kozlowski, Jonathan Rose and Jennifer Vogt
Circulation: Cathy DeGregory, Ave Maria Gonzalez, Ron Hedges and Andre Tillman

Library of Congress Cataloging-in-Publication Data
Available Upon Request

ISBN 1-56072-994-5

Copyright © 2001 by Nova Science Publishers, Inc.
227 Main Street, Suite 100
Huntington, New York 11743
Tele. 631-424-6682   Fax 631-425-5933
E Mail: Novascience@earthlink.net

All rights reserved. No part of this book may be reproduced, stored in a retrieval system or transmitted in any form or by any means: electronic, electrostatic, magnetic, tape, mechanical photocopying, recording or otherwise without permission from the publishers.

The authors and publisher have taken care in preparation of this book, but make no expressed or implied warranty of any kind and assume no responsibility for any errors or omissions. No liability is assumed for incidental or consequential damages in connection with or arising out of information contained in this book.

This publication is designed to provide accurate and authoritative information with regard to the subject matter covered herein. It is sold with the clear understanding that the publisher is not engaged in rendering legal or any other professional services. If legal or any other expert assistance is required, the services of a competent person should be sought. FROM A DECLARATION OF PARTICIPANTS JOINTLY ADOPTED BY A COMMITTEE OF THE AMERICAN BAR ASSOCIATION AND A COMMITTEE OF PUBLISHERS.

Printed in the United States of America

CONTENTS

Preface vii

North-South Korean Relations: A Chronology of the "New" Dialogue .. 1
Mark E. Manyin

North Korea-Japan Relations: The Normalization Talks and
the Compensation/Reparations Issue 13
Mark E. Manyin

North Korea's Nuclear Weapons Program 21
Larry A. Niksch

Korea: Procedural and Jurisdictional Questions Regarding Possible
Normalization of Relations with North Korea 35
Zachary S. David, Larry A. Niksch, Larry Q. Nowels, Vladimir N.
Pregelj, Rinn-Sup Shinn, Robert G. Sutter

U.S.-North Korean Relations since 1948 37

What is the Current Status of U.S.-North Korean Political Relations? 53

U.S.-North Korean Military Relations 59

Normalizing U.S. Commercial Relations with North Korea 65

Expanded Economic Assistance and Support for North Korea: What Steps Could the United States Take? 79

Nuclear Cooperation and Nonproliferation 87

Index 93

NORTH-SOUTH KOREAN RELATIONS: A CHRONOLOGY OF THE "NEW" DIALOGUE

Mark E. Manyin

BACKGROUND

The Historic June 2000 Summit. On June 13, 2000, South Korean President Kim Dae Jung flew to Pyongyang for a three-day summit with North Korea's paramount leader, Kim Jong-il. The meeting was the first-ever between the leaders of North and South Korea, which have been divided since 1945 and officially at war since 1950.[1] The two Kims signed a joint declaration pledging, among other things, to work towards eventual reunification, open a dialogue between government officials, engage in economic cooperation, permit family reunions, and engage in cultural and athletic exchanges. Upon his return to Seoul, Kim Dae Jung stated that Kim Jong-il had verbally agreed that even if North-South tensions continued to be reduced, U.S. troops should remain in South Korea to help preserve regional and peninsular stability. "It became clear," the South Korean president continued, "that we will not ever go to war again."[2]

Progress in the New Inter-Korean Dialogue. In the months that followed the summit, the two Koreas developed a new dialogue. Four rounds of interministerial talks were held, the two countries' defense

---

[1] North and South Korea's formal names are the Democratic People's Republic of Korea (DPRK) and the Republic of Korea (ROK0, respectively.
[2] *Korea Herald*, June 20, 2000.

ministers met for the first time, talks on economic cooperation commenced, the two countries marched together at the 2000 Sydney Olympics, and emotional reunions were held among hundreds of families separated by the inter-Korean divide. South Korean President Kim has stated his desire to negotiate a North-South peace agreement, which would officially end the Korean War, before he leaves office in February 2003. Moreover, numerous South Korean businesses and citizens have forged their own contacts with North Korea, a development made possible when President Kim - - under his so-called "sunshine policy" of trying to induce more cooperative behavior from North Korea through engaging Pyongyang – relaxed Seoul's previous insistence that the government monopolize all contact with the North.[3]

Setbacks. This is not to say that the dialogue has or will proceed smoothly. Several snags have been encountered along the way. After a fast start, in the fall of 2000 North Korea slowed the pace of the dialogue, leading to the postponement and delay of scheduled family reunions and several meetings. Kim Jong-il's reciprocal visit to South Korea has yet to be scheduled, making it increasingly unlikely that the tri will take place in the spring of 2001, as South Korean officials had hoped. North Korean state-run media outlets have called on U.S. troops to withdraw from South Korea, a demand reportedly also made by the DPRK defense minister during talks with the Rok in September 2000. Pyongyang has also given mixed signals in its willingness to accept Kim Dae Jung's proposal to conclude a peace treaty directly with South Korea, a move that would require the North to drop its longstanding policy of negotiating a peace only with the United States.

On the economic side, the Hyundai conglomerate's business ventures in North Korea – the economic flagships of Ki Dae Jung's sunshine policy – are encountering serious financial difficulties, in part due to the financial difficulties of Hyundai's parent corporation. Signs of an economic slowdown in South Korea have added weight to the warnings of the ROK's opposition party, the Grand National Party, that the government should avoid providing North Korea with significant economic assistance, such as the 500,000 kw of electricity Pyongyang demanded in December 2000, as a precondition for future talks.

What are North Korea's Intentions? The biggest set of questions revolve around North Korea's intentions, which remain opaque. Is its diplomatic opening a sign that Kim Jong-il has changed his stripes, deciding to adopt a more cooperative posture and possibly reform the faltering North

---

[3] For more on South Korea's "sunshine policy" toward North Korea, see CRS Report RL 30188, *South Korea's Sunshine Policy*, by Rinn-Sup- Shinn.

Korean economy? Or, are the North's actions merely tactics to obtain economic concessions from South Korea and its allies, thereby propping up North Korea's economy, rearming its deteriorating conventional military, and preserving the power of its communist elite? Events since the summit appear to support the latter interpretation. Thus far, North Korea has largely succeeded in steering the North-South dialogue toward discussions over economic assistance and away from discussions over military confidence-building measures. This has led observers in South Korea and the U.S. to criticize President Kim for conceding too much to the North without insisting on enough in return.

Criticism in South Korea. Within South Korea, the above criticism – largely from the opposition GNP – mounted in the late fall and winter of 2000. The GNP's concerns are less over the logic of Kim's sunshine policy – the party generally has come to support some form of engagement with North Korea – than over its implementation.[4] The GNP leadership has charged President Kim with failing to insist on reciprocity from Pyongyang in exchange for Seoul's concessions and with ignoring important issues such as confidence-building measures and the several hundred South Korean POWs and kidnapping victims said to remain in the North. The GNP also has criticized Kim for failing to adequately consult with the National Assembly -- in which the GNP is the largest party – and for trying to silence domestic criticism of North Korea.[5]

Nonetheless, the sheer breadth and depth of the dialogue, combined with the fact that follow-up meetings have been held and scheduled, indicates that this time Seoul and Pyongyang are making a serious attempt to regularize and institutionalize their dialogue, in contrast to previously ephemeral thaws in 1972, 1985 and the early 1990s. While the rapprochement is not yet irreversible, each subsequent meeting and contact strengthens the newly intensified process.

Implications for the U.S. The thaw on the Korean Peninsula has several important implications for the United States. First, it is likely to increase pressure on the United States, as well as Japan, to improve relations with North Korea. Second, in South Korea, the perceived reduction in the

---

[4] Lee Hoi-Chang's speech to the American Enterprise Institute, September 15, 1999.
[5] For instance, Hwang Jang Yop, the highest-ranking North Korean ever to defect to South Korea, has accused the South Korean government of threatening to evict him from a protected "safe house" in order to stop him from criticizing North Korea and Kim Dae Jung's sunshine policy. See *Yonhap*, November 23, 2000, and "The Moral Cost of Engagement," *Far Eastern Economic Review*, December 28, 2000.

North Korean military threat has created a more critical public climate regarding the presence of the 37,000 U.S. troops in South Korea, a new attitude that already has spilled over into other areas of U.S.-ROK relations. Third, public reactions to a reduction in tensions also could influence a similar debate in Japan, particularly in Okinawa, over U.S. troops in that country. Finally, many U.S. observers want economic cooperation between the Koreas to be designed in a way that will limit the North's ability to increase the resources it places into its military, including its nuclear and long-range missile programs.[6]

CHRONOLOGY

Operationally, the rapprochement process has been driven by inter-ministerial meetings among senior-level officials. Most of the broad agreements and developments since the summit have been negotiated and announced at these gatherings, with the details on implementation delegated to working level negotiators.

Upcoming Events

01/2001 - Joint research on the DPRK's electricity situation scheduled to begin.

02/06/2001 - 2nd South-North economic cooperation promotion committee meeting scheduled.

02/2001, late - 3rd family reunions scheduled.

03/2001 - 5th inter-ministerial talks scheduled. Limited mail exchanges to start.

---

[6] For further information on U.S.-Korean relations, see CRS Issue Briefs IB91141, *North Korea's Nuclear Weapons Program* and IB98045, *U.S.-South Korean Relations – Issues for Congress,* both by Larry Niksch.

Past Events – 2000

3/9/00 – Kim Dae Jung's "Berlin Declaration." In a speech in Berlin, ROK President Kim signaled Seoul's interest in extending economic assistance to North Korea, in exchange for reopening an official North-South dialogue.

4/8/00 – The ROK and DPRK announce they will hold the first-ever inter-Korean summit in June.

5/29-31/00 – DPRK leader Kim Jong-il makes a secret visit to Beijing, meeting with top Chinese leaders.

6/13-15/00 – **The North-South summit**, Pyongyang, between ROK President Ki Dae Jung (shown at left n photo) and DPRK leader Kim Jong-il. The two leaders sign a vaguely worded jointly declaration, which indicates their agreement to work toward unification, exchange visits by members of divided families around August 15, 2000, repatriate DPRK prisoners in the ROK who have completed their jail terms, work for "a balanced development" of both countries' economies, hold a dialogue between the two governments at an early date, and increase social and cultural exchanges. The declaration also mentions that Kim Jong-il accepted Kim Dae Jung's invitation to visit Seoul "at an appropriate time." After returning to South Korea, Kim Dae Jung states that Kim Jong-il verbally agreed that even if North-South tensions continued to be reduced, U.S. troops should remain in South Korea to help preserve regional and peninsular stability.

6/19/00 – The Clinton Administration eases economic sanctions imposed on North Korea since its invasion of South Korea in 1950.

7/31/00 – **ROK and DPRK foreign ministers meet** on the sidelines of the ASEAN[7] Regional Forum (ARF) in Bangkok, the first time the DPRK had been invited to the ARF. The ministers issue a joint press release agreeing to: hold ministerial-level talks starting August 29, hold family reunions, reopen liaison offices in Panmunjon, and begin discussing the reopening of severed railway links.

---

[7] Association of Southeast Asian Nations.

8/11/00 – Major ROK media publishers meet with Kim Jong-il and the state-run North Korean press in Pyongyang. The publishers agree on a plan of mutual coverage, including a pledge to "avoid confrontation . . . and stop slander."

8/15/00 – The North-South Liaison office in Panmunjon, in the Demilitarized Zone (DMZ), reopened. It had been closed by the DPRK in 1996.

8/15/00 – **200 families reunited.** 100 ROK citizens travel to Pyongyang. 100 DPRK citizens travel to Seoul.

8/23/00 – Hyundai and the DPRK reach agreement to begin construction of an industrial park in Kaesong, a DPRK town near the DMZ. Surveying is to begin in September 2000 and construction is to begin in November 2000.

8/29-9/1/00 – **2nd Interministerial Meetings**, in Pyongyang. The ministers issue a 7-point joint press statement, which included the following items: a 2nd round of family reunions is to be held by year-end; the two Red Crosses are to begin discussing the exchange of letters among divided families; discussions will begin in September over holding military-to-military meetings; and working level meetings will begin on economic cooperation and on reconnecting the Seoul-Shinuiju railroad. The next round of ministerial talks is scheduled for Sept. 27-30. The DPRK asked for 1 million tons of food aid. The end of talks are delayed a day, reportedly due to DPRK opposition to military confidence building measures, such as establishing a hotline and holding regular military-to-military talks. The communiqué did not mention a reciprocal visit to Seoul by Kim Jong-il. Prior to the meetings, there had been speculation that such a trip would take place in Nov. 2000.

9/12/00 – The ROK and DPRK announce that DPRK leader **Kim Jong-il will visit Seoul in the spring of 2001.** The announcement is made during a meeting of key aides to both leaders. The aides sign a joint communiqué stating that working level economic talks will open on September 25, defense ministers will meet, and a joint flood control survey of the Imjin River will be completed within the year.

9/17/00 – ROK President Kim's party announces its intention to revise ROK's National Security Law, which bans praise of and unauthorized contacts with DPRK.

9/18/00 – The ROK starts work on reconnecting the Seoul-Shinuiju (DPRK) railroad. The ROK's main opposition party boycotts the event.

9/19/-23/00 – Red Cross negotiators meet and agree to two more family reunions (Nov. 2-5 and Dec. 5-7, 2000) for 100 people from each side in Seoul & Pyongyang, and to allow 300 people from each Korea to exchange letters with separated families, which would be the 1st ever inter-Korean mail links.

9/25-26/00 – **1st-ever inter-Korean defense ministerial meeting**, on Cheju Island (ROK). In a joint statement, the two ministers agree to ease military tensions so as to "completely eliminate" the danger of war on the Korean peninsula. To allow the relinking of inter-Korean railroads and highways through the DMZ, the defense ministers agree to begin clearing mines and create an area of joint control in the DMZ. Another round of ministerial talks is scheduled for Nov. 2000, and a round of working level talks on the railroad is scheduled for October 2000. The DPRK did not respond to the ROK's confidence-building proposals, which included: establishing joint military committees at the working and upper levels, establishing a military hot line, and agreeing to observation and advanced notification of troop movements and exercises. Reportedly, the DPRK defense minister called on the U.S. to withdraw its troops from South Korea.

9/25-26/00 – **1st working level economic meeting**, in Seoul, makes progress on investment and double taxation agreements. ROK agrees to give DPRK 500,000 tons of food aid.

9/27-10/1/00 – **3rd interministerial talks**, on Cheju Island (ROK), end without much substantive progress. In a joint communiqué, the two Koreas agree to set up a joint economic commission and to increased social and academic exchanges. Reportedly, the DPRK requested a slowdown in the pace of inter-Korean projects.

10/1/00 – ROK President Kim proposes a "2+2" peace initiative, whereby the ROK and DPRK would sign a peace agreement that would later be endorsed and guaranteed by U.S. and China.

10/6/00 – The U.S. and DPRK sign a statement in which the DPRK declares its opposition to all forms of terrorism.

10/9-12/00 – Vice Marshal Jo Myong Rok, the DPRK's second-in-command, travels to Washington, the first visit to the U.S. by a high-level DPRK official. The two sides sign a joint communiqué, which states that "there are a variety of available means, including the four-party talks" for forging permanent peace arrangements, a move that the ROK hailed as a sign that North Korea might support President Kim's 2+2 peace treaty initiative, thereby abandoning its policy of negotiating a peace treaty only with the U.S.

10/18/00 – DPRK postpones scheduled 2nd round working level economic meetings due to its "internal situation."

10/23/00 – U.S. Secretary of State Madeleine Albright travels to the DPRK.

10/29/00 – 4th round of Ministerial-level talks are postponed.

10/31/00 – DPRK-Japan normalization talks. DPRK rejects Japan's proposal to offer it "economic aid" rather than financial "compensation" for the 40-year occupation of Korea. Future talks are not scheduled.

11/1/00 – DPRK-U.S. missile talks open.

11/2-5/00 – Scheduled family reunions are postponed.

11/6/00 – In talks with the United Nations Command (UNC) over opening the DMZ to inter-Korean rail and roads, the DPRK rejects a UNC proposal to transfer negotiating authority from the UNC to the ROK.

11/8-11/00 – **2nd round working level economic meeting**, in the DPRK, which had been scheduled for Oct. 18. Four agreement are signed, extending protection to foreign investors, ending double taxation, designating local banks to allow direct financial transactions, and establishing a bilateral body to settle potential trade disputes. Officials estimate that the agreements, which need to be ratified at the ministerial level and then by legislatures, could take 1-3 years before they go into effect. During the visit, ROK negotiators inspect a DPRK food aid distribution center, the first time the DPRK opens its distribution infrastructure to ROK inspection. The DPRK also provides a detailed accounting of food and distribution.

11/16/00 – The DPRK and the United Nations Command in Korea agree that ROK can have administrative authority over the southern portions of the DMZ, where an inter-Korean railroad and highway are to be built.

11/28/00 – In a speech in Singapore, ROK President Kim calls for reopening the Four Party talks among the two Koreas, the United States, and China as a vehicle to negotiate a peace agreement. The talks, which opened in 1997, had been stalled since the fall of 1999.

11/28/00 – **1st working level military talks** to discuss administering the construction of inter-Korean railroad and road through the DMZ.

11/30/00 – 2nd round of defense minister talks, scheduled for Nov. 2000, do not take place.

11/30-12/2/00 – **2nd round of family reunions** of 100 people from each side. The reunions, originally scheduled for early November, are a lower key affair than the 1st round in August, in part due to protests in the ROK against the cost of the 1st reunion. The reunions proceed less smoothly than the 1st round: the DPRK lashes out at the head of the ROK Red Cross for his criticism of the reunion process, and the DPRK detains an ROK reporter who had criticized the DPRK. The two Red Crosses agree that letters between families will be allowed at a future date.

12/5/00 – 3rd round family reunions, originally scheduled for this date, are postponed.

12/10/00 – ROK President Kim receives the Nobel Peace Price in Oslo.

12/11/00 – ROK President Kim says he expects to sign a far-reaching pact if DPRK leader Kim Jong-il visits Seoul in the spring of 2001.

12/12/00 – **2nd round working level military talks**, in the DMZ, produce a consensus on general principals for the repair of North-South railroads and construction of North-South roads in the DMZ. The two sides begin to draft common regulations for emergencies or accidental military conflict.

12/12-1/6/00 – **4th round inter-ministerial talks**, in Pyongyang. In a joint statement, the two sides announce: the establishment of an economic cooperation panel to meet later in December; a 3rd round of family reunions to be held in Feb. 2001 and a 5th ministerial level meeting to be held in march; work would begin on a DPRK proposal to open its East Sea waters to ROK fishermen. The talks are more contentious than previous rounds. As a prerequisite for more dialogue, the DPRK demands that the ROK agree to provide 500,000 kw of electricity. The ROK refuses, convincing the DPRK to defer the issue to economic cooperation panel meeting. The DPRK protests an ROK Defense White Paper identifying DPRK as "the main enemy," pending a substantive reduction of the DPRK military threat.

12/21/00 – **3rd Round working level military talks**, in the DMZ, produces no significant results. The DPRK did not respond to ROK proposals for details safeguards to prevent accidental clashes between the two militaries, for a hotline be set up to link the two militaries, and for the DPRK to prevent its ships from crossing the Northern Limitation Line (NLL) demarcating the two countries' sea border. The DPRK again expressed dissatisfaction about being designated as the ROK's main enemy in the ROK's Defense White Paper.

12/28/00 – **1st South-North economic cooperation promotion committee meeting,** in Pyongyang. The two sides agree to prepare a joint inspection of the DPRK's energy situation in January and to discuss joint flood control surveys of the Imjin River, which runs through the DMZ. The talks stalled at one point when the DPRK demanded that the ROK agree to provide electricity before other issues were resolved. A second meeting is scheduled for Feb. 6-8, 2001 in Seoul.

2001

1/1/01 – In joint New year's editorials in three official newspapers, the DPRK states that it will place top priority on rebuilding its economy.

1/6/01 – Radio Pyongyang, the DPRK's official station, broadcasts a lecture on Korean unification that calls for a DPRK-U.S. peace treat but omits any mention of a DPRK-ROK treaty.

1/15/01 – DPRK leader Kim Jong-il begins an unannounced trip to China, his second visit in less than a year. Reportedly, his itinerary includes stops in Shanghai's financial district and Shenzhen, China's first special economic zone.

1/17/01 – The ROK's foreign minister announces that the U.S. and ROK have reached an agreement allowing the ROK to deploy missiles with a 300 km (187 mile) range, nearly double the previous 180 km. Limit set by a 1979 bilateral agreement.

NORTH KOREA-JAPAN RELATIONS: THE NORMALIZATION TALKS AND THE COMPENSATION/REPARATIONS ISSUE

Mark E. Manyin

SUMMARY

Japan and North Korea have not established official relations since North Korea was founded in 1948. In 2000, the two countries held three rounds of normalization talks, which had been frozen since 1992. One of Pyongyang's key demands is that Tokyo compensates North Korea for Japan's colonization of the Korean Peninsula from 1910-1945. Though Japan has resisted using terms such as "compensation" and "reparations." Tokyo has offered to provide North Korea with a large-scale economic aid package much as it gave south Korea economic assistance when Tokyo and Seoul normalized relations in 1965. North Korea, however, insists that it will only accept "compensation". This disagreement over terminology has contributed to the current deadlock in the normalization negotiations.

The 1965 Japan-South Korean settlement consisted of a $300 million grant, $200 million in low-interest long-term government loans, and $300 million in private credits from Japanese financial institution. There are a number of estimates for the present value of the 1965 Japan-South Korea settlement, ranging from as low as $3.4 billion to over $20 billion. One methodology that adjusts for inflation in Japan and for inter-Korean population differences yields a 1999 value of approximately $3.8 billion.

Reportedly, Japanese officials are discussing a package on the order of $5-$10 billion.

This report will be updated periodically to track developments in the Japan-North Korea normalization talks.

BACKGROUND

In the fall of 1999, William Perry, Special Advisor to the President on North Korea, unveiled a new strategy for halting North Korea's nuclear weapons and long-range missile programs.[8] One of the "carrots" in the United States' policy appears to be a prospective large-scale economic assistance package, conditional upon North Korea's cooperation.[9] It is widely believed that one of the largest source of economic aid to Pyongyang would come from a prospective Japanese offer of monetary "compensation" for its colonization of the Korean peninsula in the first half of the 20th Century.[10] To this end, South Korea and the Clinton Administration – the former under its so-called "sunshine policy" toward North Korea – urged Japan to reduce tensions with North Korea.[11] Tokyo and Pyongyang have not established official relations since North Korea was founded in 1948. North Korea insists that before it will establish relations with Tokyo, Japan must provide an apology and monetary compensation to resolve Japan's past treatment of Korea.[12] Japan has agreed in principle to offer an economic package to North Korea, but has been vague about its amount, form, timing, and characterization.

---

[8] See William J. Perry, "Review of United States Policy Toward North Korea," Unclassified Report, October 12, 1999, available at [http://www.state.gov/www/regions/eap/991012_northkorea_rpt.html].

[9] "Japan's Approach to DPRK Viewed," *SISA Journal*, November 18, 1999, translated by the Foreign Broadcast Information Service, FTS 19991128000519.

[10] Marcus Noland, "The Economics of Korean Unification," prepared for *Foresight Magazine*, February 2000, available at [http://www.iie.com/TESTMONY/foresigh.htm]. Victor Cha, "DPRK Dialogue," *Comparative Connections*, 4th Quarter 1999, [http://www.csis.org/pacfor/cc].

[11] "Seoul Urges Tokyo to Compensate Pyongyang for Colonial Rule," *Korea Herald*, May 7, 199. For a detailed discussion of South Korea's sunshine policy, see Rinn-Sup Shinn, *South Korea: "Sunshine Policy" and its Political Context*, CRS Report RL 30188.

[12] See, for example, "Text of North Korean Government Statement against Japan," *BBC*, August 13, 1999.

In 2000, North Korea improved relations with all the major countries in Northeast Asia, with the exception of Japan. Most dramatically, South Korean President Kim Dae Jung and North Korean leader Kim Jong-il held the first-ever inter-Korean summit meeting in mid-June. The two leaders pledged to take steps toward an eventual reunification, including setting up economic cooperation projects between the two Koreas. Two weeks before the summit, Kim Jong-il traveled to Beijing, his first trip to China since the death of his father and predecessor, Kim Il-Sung, in 1994. Shortly after the summit, the U.S. lifted most of its remaining economic sanctions on North Korea. In July 2000, Russian President Vladimir Putin visited North Korea, signaling a thaw in Moscow-Pyongyang relations, which have been icy, since the Soviet Union established relations with South Korea in 1990. These diplomatic moves by North Korea have placed even great pressures on Tokyo to improve relations with Pyongyang.

THE JAPAN-NORTH KOREA NORMALIZATION TALKS – ISSUES AND CHRONOLOGY

Disagreements over the Economic Settlement Package. Regarding the size of Japan's economic package to North Korea, either side has not released official figures, though Pyongyang reportedly has demanded $10 billion at minimum. Some Japanese experts believed that North Korea will ask for a settlement in the $20 billion range. According to Japanese North Korea-watchers, no consensus has been reached in Tokyo on Japan's bottom line, though there have been reports that Japanese officials are discussing a package on the order of $5-$10 billion. According to one report in the Japanese press, Japanese officials in October 2000 were considering a $9 billion package.[13] Observers suggest that Tokyo will argue that $2 billion be deducted from the final amount in order to give Japan credit for its $1 billion contribution to the Korean Peninsula Energy Development Organization (KEDO) and the $1 billion North Korea owes Japanese sources (mainly Japanese banks) from unpaid debts incurred in the 1970s and 1980s.[14]

In addition to the size of the settlement, the two sides have clashed over terminology. Japan is refusing North Korea's demand that the package be

---

[13] Tokyo Shimbun, October 26, 2000.
[14] Author's conversations with Japanese North Korea experts following CRS Workshop, "Dealing with North Korea," March 2, 2000; see also Cha, "DPRK Dialogue."

labeled as "reparations," or even "compensation." Instead, Tokyo has offered to characterize the monies as "economic assistance," as it did in the 1965 Japan-South Korean normalization negotiations.[15] This semantic dispute has momentarily stalled the talks. Other issues likely to be contentious include the conditions placed on Pyongyang's use of the aid/reparations, and the composition of the money – grants or loans.[16] Additionally, North Korea is demanding that Japan issue a formal, "legally binding apology" from the Japanese emperor and/or Prime Minister. Japan has countered that a sufficient apology was extended as part of 1995 statement by then Prime Minister Tomiichi Murayama expressing regret for Japan's past actions.

Other Contentious Issues. Any normalization agreement will be politically difficult for the Japanese government. In recent years, relations with North Korea have become a high-profile political issue in Japan, due to North Korea's 1998 Taepodong missile launch over Japan, its 1999 naval incursion into Japanese waters, and the release of new (albeit unconfirmed) evidence that Pyongyang kidnapped Japanese citizens in the 1970s and 1980s.[17] Public opinion polls indicate that most Japanese favor adopting a cautious approach toward North Korea.[18] Conservative groups in Japan – including many members of the dominant Liberal Democratic Party – opposed the government's decisions in March and October 2000 to resume shipments of food aid to North Korea, arguing that Japanese assistance should be conditioned on Pyongyang's cooperation on the abduction cases and on missile and nuclear weapons issues.[19] An additional concern expressed by these groups is that Japanese compensation or food aid might be used for North Korea's military rather than for its populace. During the April 2000 talks, the Japanese delegation also raised the issues of North

---

[15] "Kono Confirms Offering Economic Cooperation to N. Korea," *Kyodo*, August 25, 2000. Japan's position is that since it has never been at war with North Korea, it is not required to pay reparations.

[16] Cha, "DPRK Dialogue."

[17] For more n how the North Korea threat has caused many Japanese policymakers to rethink Japan's defense posture, see Richard Cronin, *Japan's Changing Security Outlook*, CRS Report RL30256, July 9, 1999. See also Rinn-Sup Shinn, *North Korea: A Chronology of Provocations, 1950-2000,* March 15, 2000.

[18] According to a 2000 poll, only 36% of Japanese surveyed believed Japan should resume food aid to North Korea, compared with 51% in August 1997. *Mainichi Shimbun,* February 27, 2000.

[19] ON March 7, 200, Japan announced its intention to deliver 100,000 tons of rice to North Korea, its first shipment since the food aid program was suspended following Pyongyang's launch of a two-stage Taepodong missile over Japan in August 1998. In October 2000, Japan announced it would send an additional 500,000 tons of rice aid to North Korea.

Korea's alleged drug trafficking, and its alleged biological and chemical weapons programs.

The 9th Round (April 2000). In the April 2000 Japan-North Korea talks, North Korea insisted that relations be normalized only after completing a "settlement of the past," a phrase Pyongyang defines to include four items: an apology, compensation, the return of cultural assets taken from Korea during the occupation, and the granting of legal status to ethnic Koreans living in Japan. For future negotiating rounds, North Korea proposed establishing panels to deal with other outstanding issues, including Pyongyang's missile development program and the whereabouts of ten Japanese allegedly kidnapped by North Korean agents. Japan, seeking to avoid decoupling the compensation/apology issue from the kidnapping and missile disputes, rejected the North Korean proposal.

The 10th Round (August 2000). On July 26, 2000, the Japanese and North Korean Foreign Minister staged an unprecedented meeting at the ASEAN Regional Forum meeting in Bangkok. The two officials agreed to hold another round of talks in Tokyo in August. They also agreed to resume discussions over further visitations to Japan by women who married Korean husbands and immigrated to North Korea.

At the August 21-24, 2000 bilateral meetings in Japan for the first time formally raised the possibility of providing an economic assistance package – *i.e.* not a compensation payment – to North Korea. Reportedly, no figures were discussed, and North Korea did not respond to the offer. The two sides agreed to hold another round of talks in a third country in October, with a goal of establishing diplomatic ties by the end of 2000. The negotiators also agreed to expand bilateral contacts to include politicians and business enterprises, and to set up committees to handle two of North Korea's demands: the return of cultural treasures taken from Korea during the Japanese occupation, and improving the legal status of Koreans living in Japan. Reportedly, North Korea asked Japan to resume trade insurance and full-scale economic aid, but Japanese negotiators declined.

The 11th Round October 2000). Almost no progress was achieved during the October 30-November 1, 2000 bilateral meetings in Beijing. Reportedly, North Korea flatly rejected Japan's proposal to offer economic assistance in lieu of compensation. Japan again turned down North Korea's demand that the abduction issue is discussed outside the normalization talks. A sign of the deadlock is that the two sides did not set a date for the next round of talks.

JAPAN'S 1965 ECONOMIC AID PACKAGE TO SOUTH KOREA

On June 22, 1965, Japan and South Korea signed a Treaty of Basic Relations, normalizing relations between the two countries for the first time since Japan annexed the Korean peninsula in 1910. As part of the final settlement, Japan agreed to provide South Korea with a total sum of $800 million[20], which consisted of: a) an outright grant of $300 million, to be distributed over a 10-year period; b) a $200 million loan to be distributed over a 10-year period and repaid over 20 years at 3.5% interest; c) $300 million in private credits over 10 years from Japanese banks and financial institutions.

Prior to the 1965 agreement, the normalization negotiations between Tokyo and Seoul had dragged on for over fourteen years, and had triggered strong emotions in both countries. Throughout the 1950s, South Korean President Syngman Rhee adopted a confrontational approach toward Japan, and successive Japanese governments showed little enthusiasm for accepting Rhee's demands that Japan apologize and compensate for its colonization of the Korean peninsula.

Relations warmed dramatically following a military coup in 1961, led by general park Chung-Hee, who established rapid industrialization – following the Japanese model of export-led development – as his country's paramount economic goal. To this end, Park was eager for Japanese economic assistance, and adopted conciliatory postures on most outstanding issues. The approximate size and composition of the compensation package was one of the first issue to be resolved following Park's coup. The South Korean side, which at one point had asked for as much as $2 billion, lowered its demands to $700 million in grant aid before agreeing to the $800 million total package. Reportedly, until late 1962, Japan had offered only $70 million in total compensation, a figure the U.S. State Department at the time described as "unrealistically low."[21] Furthermore, the Treaty on Basic Relations did not contain any reference to a Japanese apology. Instead, Japan's reparation payments was characterized as "economic assistance."

---

[20] According to the South Korean Ministry of Foreign Affairs and Trade, the aid was distributed in dollars, not yen.

[21] *Foreign Relations of the United States, 1961-1963, volume XXII (Northeast Asia)*, 567-69; Chong-Sik Lee, *Japan and Korea: The Political Dimension* (Stanford, CA: Hoover Institution Press, 1985), 50.

The terms of the Treaty enraged many south Koreans. Charging that the agreement amounted to a "sellout," Korea's opposition parties boycotted the ratification process in the National Assembly. Violent anti-government protests erupted throughout the country, and the Park government imposed marital law to suppress anti-government protests around the country, the second time in less than a year troops were mobilized to curtail protests against the government's Japan policy. The agreement also faced strong but eventually ineffectual opposition in Japan, where the Socialist party – which had friendly ties with North Korea – argued that the Treaty would impede Korean unification and was a prelude to an anti-Communist alliance in Asia.[22]

ESTIMATING THE PRESENT VALUE OF THE 1965 SETTLEMENT

There are a wide range of estimates for the present value of the 1965 Japan-South Korea settlement. At the low end is a method that adjusts for inflation in the U.S. economy, yielding a value of approximately $3,4 billion in 1999 dollars.[23] At the high end is a calculation that produces a value of $20 billion in today's dollars by adjusting for inflation in the Japanese economy, appreciation of the yen, accrued interest, and differences in population in North and south Korea.[24] One methodology that adjusts for Japanese inflation since 1965 and for inter-Korean population differences yields a present value of ¥418 billion ($3.8 billion using an exchange rate of

---

[22] Lee, *Japan and Korea*, 55.
[23] This method uses the U.S. gross domestic product (GDP) deflator to adjust for inflation between 1965 and 1999. The GDP deflator is the ratio of nominal GDP in a given year to real GDP in that same year. In 1999 the GDP deflator was 104.37 (1996 = 100), 4.35 times the 1965 deflator of 23.98. Thus, $800 million in 1965 dollars would be worth approximately $3.4 billion in1999 dollars.
[24] Noland, "The Economics of Korean Unification." For his accrued interest adjustment, Noland assumes an annual rate of return of 5%. Noland acknowledges that the Japanese side is likely to reject the notion of adjusting for accrued interest, on the grounds that North Korea's intransigence is to blame for the Perennially stalemated normalization talks. March 2000 conversation between Marcus Noland and the author. According tot he U.S. Census Bureau, in 1965, North Korea's population was approximately 11.9 million, approximately 40% the size of south Korea's population of 28.7 million in the same year. In 1999, North Korea's population was estimated to be 21.4 million, around 45% the south Korean total of 47 million.

¥110 = $1). If the same disbursement formula used in 1965 were applied today, the ¥418 billion would break out as ¥157 billion ($1.42 billion) in outright grants, ¥104 billion ($950 million) in concessionary government loans, and ¥157 billion ($1.42 billion) in private credits.[25]

The above figures should be interpreted as rough approximations. Computing the present value of a past sum is an inherently inexact task. When more than one country is involved, the calculation is made even less precise by long-term changes and short-term fluctuations in exchange rates. Additionally, an exact calculation would take into account differences between North Korea and South Korea, including the extent of the claims for damage by the Japanese occupation. Finally, the adjustments are made for the total figure of $800 million, even though the actual value of Japan's compensation package was lower: Over 60% ($500 million) of the settlement was disbursed as government loans and private credits, which are less valuable to the recipient than outright grants. Thus, the calculations presented, although providing a preliminary comparative baseline, tend to overstate the present value of Japan's settlement with South Korea.

On the other hand, the 1965 settlement occurred before the revelation that Japan had forcibly used tens of thousands of Korean "comfort women" to provide sexual services to Japanese soldiers during World War II. North Korea is insisting that Japan's compensation take into account the comfort women's plight, a demand that (if it is met) presumably would raise the value of the settlement package.[26]

---

[25] This method uses the Japanese GDP deflator to adjust for inflation between 1965 and 1999. In 1999 the Japanese GDP deflator was approximately 3.5 times the size of the deflator in 1965. Using this figure, the 1965 compensation package of Y288 billion would be worth roughly ¥1.01 trillion today ($9.2 billion, at ¥110 = $1). To adjust for population differences, multiply ¥1.01 trillion by 0.41, which is the ratio of North Korea's 1965 population (11.9 million) to South Korea's 1965 population (28.7million). The result is ¥418 billion ($3.8 billion).

[26] *Yomiuri Shimbun*, April 8, 2000.

NORTH KOREA'S NUCLEAR WEAPONS PROGRAM

Larry A. Niksch

SUMMARY

North Korea's nuclear weapons program became an immediate foreign policy issue facing the United States because of North Korea's refusal to carry out its obligations under the Nuclear Non-Proliferation Treaty (NPT) and other nuclear accords it had signed. North Korea has constructed nuclear reactors and a plutonium reprocessing plant at a site called Yongbyon. U.S. and other foreign intelligence assessments have concluded that North Korea probably has acquired enough weapons-grade plutonium for the manufacture of at least one nuclear weapon.

The Clinton Administration attempted to arrange "comprehensive negotiations" with North Korea over the issue and other issues between North Korea and the United States; but North Korea's violation of its obligations under the NPT aborted such talks until August 1994.

The United States and North Korea signed an agreement on October 21, 1994, that offers North Korea a package of benefits in return for a freeze of North Korea's nuclear program. Benefits to North Korea include: light water nuclear reactors totaling 2,000 electric megawatts by the year 2003; shipments of "heavy oil" to North Korea (50,000 tons in 1995 and 500,000 tons annually beginning in 1996 until the first light water reactor is built).

Dismantlement of North Korea's current nuclear facilities and a resolution of the International Atomic Energy Agency (IAEA) demand for a special inspection of suspected nuclear waste sites are postponed for at least five years by the Agreed Framework. The same is true of North Korean consent to the removal of reactor fuel rods, which North Korea removed from its operating reactor in May 1994. The United States has faced several policy problems since the signing of the Agreed Framework, including securing approximately $60 million annually to finance heavy oil shipments to North Korea, evidence of clandestine North Korean nuclear activities, and North Korea's development of long range missiles.

MOST RECENT DEVELOPMENTS

Recent high-level U.S.-North Korea negotiations, including Secretary of State Albright's visit to North Korea in October 2000, apparently made no progress in resolving the issue of verification that North Korea does not have secret nuclear weapons facilities. The visit of a North Korean General to Washington and Secretary of State Albright's visit to North Korea in October 2000 focused on U.S. efforts to negotiate a termination of North Korea's missile program. The talks made little apparent progress. The journal *Nucleonics Week* reported in its October 19, 2000 issue that the Clinton Administration considered a proposal to amend the 1994 U.S.-North Korean Agreed Framework that would have eliminated one of the two light water nuclear reactors which the United States is obligated to provide North Korea; a conventional electric power plan would be substituted. The report (substantiated by subsequent reports from other sources) stated that the Administration had discussed the prospective proposal with Japan and South Korea.

BACKGROUND AND ANALYSIS

NORTH KOREA'S NUCLEAR PROGRAM

From the U.S. standpoint, a key purpose of the U.S.-North Korean Agreed Framework of October 21, 1994 is to address the North Korean nuclear program, especially the potential of that program to produce nuclear weapons. North Korea has several nuclear facilities which have the potential to produce nuclear weapons. Most are located at Yongbyon, 60 miles of the North Korean capital of Pyongyang. The key installations are:

- An atomic reactor, with a capacity of about 5 electrical megawatts, constructed between 1980 and 1987: it reportedly is capable of expending enough uranium fuel to produce about 7 kilograms of plutonium annually – enough for the manufacture of a single atomic bomb annually. North Korea in 1989 shut down the reactor for about 70 days; U.S. intelligence agencies believe that North Korea removed fuel rods from the reactor at that time for reprocessing into plutonium suitable for nuclear weapons. In May 1994, North Korea shut down the reactor and removed about 8,000 fuel rods. Which could be reprocessed into enough plutonium for 4-5 nuclear weapons.

- Two large (estimated 50 electrical megawatts and 200 electrical megawatts) atomic reactors under construction since 1984: According to U.S. Ambassador Robert Gallucci, these plants, if completed, would be capable of producing enough spent fuel annually for 200 kilograms of plutonium, sufficient to manufacture nearly 30 atomic bombs a year.

- A plutonium reprocessing building abut 600 feet long and several stories high: Hans Blix, head of the international Atomic Energy Agency (IAEA), said after his visit to North Korea in May 1992 that the facility fit the definition of a plutonium reprocessing plant where weapons grade Plutonium – 239 is separated from a reactor's spent fuel. North Korea completed one reprocessing line in 1993. IAEA inspectors in arch 1994 saw evidence that North Korea was constructing a second reprocessing system in the building, which would double plutonium production capacity.

Satellite photographs reportedly also show that the atomic reactors have no attached power lines, which they would have if used for electric power generation. Hans Blix and a number of U.S. and South Korean experts have speculated that North Korea might have built a hidden "pilot" plutonium reprocessing laboratory as a prototype for the large reprocessing installation.

Persons interviewed for this study believe that North Korea developed the two reactors and the apparent reprocessing plant with its own resources and technology. It is believed that Kim Chong-il, the son and successor of President Kim Il-Sung who died in July 1994, directs the program, and that the military and the Ministry of Public Security (North Korea's version of the KGB) implement it. North Korea reportedly ahs about 3,000 scientists and research personnel devoted to the Yongbyon program. Many have studied nuclear technology (though not necessarily nuclear weapons production) in the Soviet Union and China and reportedly Pakistan. The training of nuclear scientists at North Korean universities reportedly is intense. North Korea has uranium deposits, estimated at 26 million tons. North Korea is believed to have one uranium producing mine.

Disclosure of the Kumchangri Underground Complex

U.S. intelligence agencies reportedly became aware of the Kumchangri underground facility in the second half of 1996. The Defense Intelligence Agency (DIA) reportedly prepared a classified report at the end of 1997, which concluded that the facility, located about 25 miles north of Yongbyon, "possibly could be a nuclear weapons-related facility by 2003." The report stated that: "The function of this site has not been determined, but it could be intended as a nuclear production and/or storage site." The DIA began to brief staff members of key congressional committees concerning the Kumchangri site in the spring of 1998. According to staffers privy to the briefing, the DIA over several months provided detailed information indicating that North Korea was constructing a nuclear installation. In August 1998, the New York Times and the Washington Post revealed the intelligence findings. Press reports also indicated that U.S. intelligence agencies are monitoring at least ten more North Korean installations of a suspicious nature. The Clinton Administration responded to the disclosure by pressuring North Korea to allow the United States access to the Kumchangri facility. An agreement was reached on March 16, 1999, providing for multiple inspections of the site in return for at least 500,000 tons of new U.S. food aid for North Korea. The first visit took place in may 1999. Administration officials declared that no evidence of nuclear activity was found. However, previous reports indicated that North Korea had removed equipment from the facility.

International Assistance

Knowledgeable individuals believe that the Soviet Union did not assist directly in the development of Yongbyon in the 1980s. The USSR provided North Korea with a small research reactor in the 1960s, which also is at Yongbyon. However, North Korean nuclear scientists continued to receive training in the USSR up to the demise of the Soviet Union in December 1991. East German and Russian nuclear and missile scientists reportedly are in North Korea. Russian military officials confirmed the presence of Russian nuclear and missile scientists inside North Korea in January 1994. In 1999 and early 2000, reports appeared that U.S. intelligence agencies had information that China was supplying important components and raw materials for North Korea's missile program.

North Korea's Delivery Systems

North Korea is developing missiles believed capable of delivering nuclear warheads. In June and July 1998, Secretary of Defense Cohen and other U.S. military officials disclosed that North Korea had succeeded in developing a "Nodong" missile with a range estimated at 600 miles, capable of covering south Korea and part of Japan. North began deploying Nodong missiles in late 1998. Since March 1994, U.S. intelligence agencies have reported that North Korea was developing two longer range Taepo Dong ballistic missiles whose range likely would include, in the first stage, all of Japan including Okinawa and, in the second stage, U.S. territories in the Western Pacific and possibly Alaska and Hawaii. On August 31, 1998, North Korea test fired a three stage rocket, apparently the prototype of the Taepo Don-1; the third stage apparently was an attempt to launch a satellite. U.S intelligence estimates reportedly concluded that such a missile would have the range to reach Alaska, Guam, and the Northern Marianas Commonwealth. Reports in early 2000 cited U.S. intelligence findings that, without further flight tests, North Korea could deploy an intercontinental ballistic missile that would be capable of striking Alaska, Hawaii, and the U.S. west coast.

These projections led the Clinton Administration to press North Korea for a new round of talks over North Korea's missile program. In talks held in March 1999 and July 2000, North Korea demanded $1 billion annually in exchange for a promise not to export missiles. North Korea said to U .S. negotiators that it would not negotiate on its missile development/deployment program, apparently contradicting the offer reported by Russian President Vladimir Putin in July 2000. U.S. negotiators reportedly rejected North Korea's demand for $1 billion but offered a lifting of U.S. economic sanctions against North Korea in exchange for an agreement on missiles. This laid the ground for the Berlin agreement of September 1999 in which North Korea agreed to defer further missile tests in return for the lifting of major U.S. economic sanctions.

STATE OF NUCLEAR WEAPONS DEVELOPMENT

U.S. and foreign intelligence agencies and experts have concluded a high range of likelihood that North Korea has acquired enough plutonium and has developed significant technology to produce a small number of nuclear weapons. North Korea's approximately 70 day shutdown of the five megawatt reactor in 1989 gave it the opportunity to remove nuclear fuel rods, from which plutonium is reprocessed. State Department officials estimate that North Korea may have acquired six to eight kilograms of plutonium from the five megawatt reactor at Yongbyon, enough, they say, for possibly one bomb. However, the U.S. Central Intelligence Agency and the Defense Intelligence Agency reportedly estimated in late 1993 that North Korea extracted enough fuel rods for about 12 kilograms of plutonium – sufficient for one or two atomic bombs. The CIA and DIA apparently base their estimate on the 1989 shutdown of the five megawatt reactor. David Albright of the Institute for Science and International Security produced in 1994 a detailed study of the 1989 reactor shutdown and concluded that if North Korea removed all of the fuel rods from the reactor during the shutdown, the rods would have contained 14 kilograms of plutonium.

South Korean and Japanese intelligence estimates reportedly are higher: 16-24 kilograms (Japan) and 7-22 kilograms (South Korea). These estimates reportedly are based on the view that North Korea could have acquired a higher volume of plutonium from the 1989 reactor shutdown and the view of a higher possibility that North Korea removed fuel rods during the 1990 and 1991 reactor slowdowns. Russian Defense Ministry analyses of late 1993 reportedly came to a similar estimate of about 20 kilograms of plutonium, enough for 2 or 3 atomic bombs. Some individual U.S. Government experts believe that under optimum conditions, North Korea could have produced close to 20 kilograms of plutonium since 1989.

There also is emerging a body of analysis suggesting that North Korea could produce more nuclear weapons from a given amount of plutonium than standard intelligence estimates have believed. State Department and U.S. intelligence estimates of the plutonium/bomb production ratio are close to the IAEA standard that a non-nuclear state would need about eight kilograms of plutonium to produce a nuclear bomb. However, IAEA spokesman, David Kyd, stated in August 1994 that Agency officials have known for some time that the eight kilogram standard was too high. He said that the IAEA retained it because of the wishes of member governments.

Kyd was reacting to a report of the National Resources Defense Council. Using North Korea as a standard non-nuclear state, the report concluded that a non-nuclear state with "low technology" could produce a one kiloton bomb (a small atomic bomb but "with the potential to kill tens of thousands of people") with three kilograms of plutonium. A non-nuclear state with "medium technology" could produce a one kiloton bomb with 1.5 kilograms of plutonium.

Before the National Resources Defense Council released the report, the U.S. Department of Energy in January 1994 lowered its mean estimate of plutonium required for a small atomic bomb from eight to four kilograms. Secretary of Defense Perry suggested in July 1994 that, with a higher level of technology that believed, North Korea could produce more nuclear weapons with a given amount of plutonium: "If they had a very advanced technology, they could make five bombs out of the amount of plutonium we estimate they have."

Russian and U.S. intelligence agencies also reportedly have learned of significant technological advances by North Korea towards nuclear weapons production. On March 10, 1992, the Russian newspaper *Argumenty I Fakty* (Arguments and Facts) published the text of a 1990 Soviet KGB report to the Soviet Central Committee on North Korea's nuclear program. It was published again by *Izvestiya* of June 24, 1994. The KGB report asserted that "According to available data, development of the first nuclear device has been completed at the DPRK nuclear research center in Yongbyon." The North Korean Government, the report stated, had decided not to test the device in order to avoid international detection. In July and December 1993 respectively, the journal *Nucleonics* (July 8) and NBC News reported that North Korea had converted reprocessed plutonium from a liquid form to pure metal, apparently prior to 1993. Nuclear experts describe this action as the last step prior to the final assembly of an atomic bomb.

Additionally, there are a number of reports and evidence that point to at least a middle range likelihood that North Korea may have smuggled plutonium from Russia. In June 1994, the head of Russia's Counterintelligence Service (successor to the KGB) said at a press conference that North Korea's attempts to smuggle "components of nuclear arms production" from Russia caused his agency "special anxiety." In August 1994, members of Germany's parliament and Chancellor Kohl's intelligence coordinator stated that they had been briefed that a German citizen arrested in May 1994 with a small amount of plutonium, smuggled from Russia, had connections with North Korea. U.S. executive branch officials have expressed concern in background briefings over the possibility that North Korea has smuggled plutonium from Russia. One U.S. official, quoted in the Washington Times, July 5, 1994, asserted that "There is the possibility that things having gotten over the [Russian-North Korea] border without anybody being aware of it." The most specific claim came in the German news magazine Stern in march 1993, which cited Russian Counterintelligence Service reports that North Korea had smuggled 56 kilograms of plutonium (enough for 7-9 atomic bombs) from Russia.

Other evidence, albeit circumstantial, includes numerous reports in 1994 by the Director of the FBI that Russian criminal organizations "may already have the capability to steal nuclear weapons, nuclear weapons components or weapons-grade material"; the close connections that North Korean intelligence and military organs have had with the former KGB and elements of the Soviet/Russian military; the network of agents North Korea is known to have inside Russia; and the publicized North Korean attempts – some apparently successful according to Russian military officials – to recruit soviet/Russian nuclear experts, including missile experts capable of designing nuclear warheads. The Japanese newspaper, SANKEI SHIMBUN, reported on June 9, 1996, that Ki Chong-u, a leading North Korean economic official, asserted in a meeting with State Department officials on April 26, 1996, that South Korea and Japan would have to deal with four North Korean missiles with nuclear warheads if they didn't provide North Korea with food.

In March 2000, President Clinton notified congress that he could not certify that North Korea was not acquiring enriched uranium for the production of nuclear weapons. The Japanese newspaper, *Sankei Shimbun*, reported on June 9, 2000, the contents of a "detailed report" from Chinese government sources on a secret North Korean uranium enrichment facility inside North Korea's Mount Chonma.

DIPLOMATIC BACKGROUND TO THE AGREED FRAMEWORK AND AMENDMENT AGREEMENTS

In 1991, the Bush Administration took several actions aimed at securing from North Korea adherence to Pyongyang's obligations as a signatory of the Nuclear Non-Proliferation Treaty (NPT); North Korea had signed the treaty in 1985. Bush Administration actions included the withdrawl of U.S. nuclear weapons from South Korea in late 1991. North Korea entered into two agreements, which specified nuclear obligations. In a denuclearization agreement signed in December 1991, North Korea and south Korea pledged not to possess nuclear weapons, not to possess plutonium reprocessing uranium enrichment facilities, and to negotiate a mutual nuclear inspection system. In January 1992, North Korea signed a safeguard agreement with the International Atomic Energy Agency (IAEA), providing for regular IAEA inspections of nuclear facilities. In 1992, North Korea rebuffed south Korea regarding implementation of the denuclearization agreement, but it did allow the IAEA to conduct six inspections during June 1992-February 1993.

In late 1992, the IAEA found evidence that North Korea had reprocessed more plutonium than the 80 grams it had disclosed to the Agency. In February 1993, the IAEA invoked a provision in the safeguard agreement and called for a "special inspection" of two concealed but apparent nuclear waste sites at Yongbyon. The IAEA believed that a special inspection would uncover information on the amount of plutonium which North Korea had produced since 1989. North Korea rejected the IAEA request and announced on March 12, 1993, an intention to withdraw from the NPT.

The NPT withdrawal threat led to low and higher level diplomatic talks between North Korea and the Clinton Administration. North Korea "suspended" its withdrawal from the NPT when the Clinton Administration agreed to a high-level meeting in June 1993. However, North Korea continued to refuse both special inspections and IAEA regular inspections of facilities designated under the safeguards agreement. In may 1994, North Korea refused to allow the IAEA to inspect the 8,000 fuel rods, which it had removed from the five megawatt reactor. In June 1994, North Korea's President Kim Il-Sung reactivated a longstanding invitation former U.S. President Jimmy Carter to visit Pyongyang. Kim offered Carter a freeze of North Korea's nuclear facilities and operations. Kim took this initiative after China reportedly informed him that it would not veto a first round of economic sanctions, which the Clinton Administration had proposed to members of the U.N. Security Council.

The Clinton Administration reacted to Kim's proposal by dropping its sanctions proposal and entering into a new round of high-level negotiations with North. This negotiation led to the Agreed Framework of October 21, 1994. Two amending agreements were concluded in 1995: a U.S.-North Korean statements in Kuala Lumpur, Malaysia in June and a supply contract for the provision of nuclear reactors to North Korea, concluded in December.

THE AGREED FRAMEWORK: PROVISIONS, IMPLEMENTATION, COSTS, FUTURE ISSUES

U.S. Objectives: Primacy to the Freeze of North Korea's Nuclear Program

The heart of the Agreed Framework and the amending accords in a deal under which the United States will provide North Korea with a package of nuclear, energy, economic, and diplomatic benefits; in return North Korea will halt the operations and infrastructure development of its nuclear program. The Agreed Framework commits North Korea to "freeze its graphite-moderated reactors and related facilities" within one month of October 21 with the freeze to be monitored by the IAEA. Ambassador Robert Gallucci, who negotiated for the United States, stated that "related facilities" include the plutonium reprocessing plant. According to Gallucci, the freeze includes a halt to construction of the 50 and 200 megawatt reactors and a North Korean promise not to refuel the five megawatt reactor. The Agreed Framework also commits North Korea to "cooperate" with the United States in finding a way to store the fuel rods removed from the five megawatt reactor in May 1994 "in a safe manner that does not involve reprocessing in the DPRK [North Korea]." Administration officials reportedly have said that a secret "confidential minute" to the Agreed Framework prohibits North Korea from construction of new nuclear facilities elsewhere in North Korea.

Gallucci and other officials have emphasized that the key policy objective of the Clinton Administration has been to secure a freeze of North Korea's nuclear program in order to prevent North Korea from producing large quantities of nuclear weapons grade plutonium through the operations of the 50 and 200 megawatt reactors and the plutonium reprocessing plant at

Yongbyon. Gallucci has referred to the prospect of North Korea of producing enough plutonium annually for nearly 30 nuclear weapons if the 50 and 200 megawatt reactors went into operation. The Administration's fear is that North Korea would have the means to export atomic bombs to other states and possess a nuclear missile capability that would threaten Japan and U.S. territories in the Pacific Ocean. The freeze, thus, is intended to attain U.S. policy goals related to nuclear non-proliferation and the NPT and prevent the emergence of a significant regional nuclear security threat.

However, the Agreed Framework does not resolve the question of North Korea's existing achievements regarding the production and acquisition of plutonium and the production of nuclear weapons. The freeze will not prevent North Korea from producing a few nuclear weapons if, according to the U.S. and foreign intelligence reports cited earlier, North Korea has enough plutonium, sufficient technology to manufacture them, and hidden facilities such as a pilot plutonium reprocessing laboratory, about which IAEA Director Blix and others have speculated. Pyongyang's continued small stockpile option appears to be a major weakness of the Agreed Framework. This would not constitute the broad strategic threat cited by Administration officials. However, a small nuclear stockpile would represent a new, dangerous element to the military situation on the Korean peninsula itself, if North Korean leaders concluded that possession of nuclear weapons provided them with insurance against unacceptable losses if they undertook a more militarily aggressive strategy toward South Korea.

Benefits to North Korea

Total U.S. Cost Projections. In December 1994, Ambassador Gallucci told the Senate Foreign Relations Committee that the cost to the United States in implementing the Agreed Framework would be in the "tens of millions of dollars." Secretary of State Christopher estimated $20-$30 million annually in testimony before the Foreign Relations Committee.

Light Water Nuclear Reactors. North Korea is to receive two light water reactors (LWRs) with a generating capacity of approximately 2,000 megawatts. The Agreed Framework set a "target date" of 2003. The United States is obligated to organize an international consortium arrangement for the acquisition and financing of the reactors. The Administration and the governments of South Korea, Japan, and other countries established in march 1995 the Korean Peninsula Energy Development Organization (KEDO) to coordinate the provision of the LWRs. North Korea initially rejected negotiating with either KEDO or South Korea over the LWR project, demanding that it deal only with the United States and that it would accept only U.S. reactors. North Korea and the United States reached an agreement in Kuala Lumpur, Malaysia, In June 1995 under which North Korea agreed to negotiate with KEDO. The Kuala Lumpur agreement left South Korea's role in the project unclear. However, South Korea's role has become apparent because of South Korea's participation in subsequent KEDO-north Korea negotiations, which concluded a supply contract in December 1995 and follow-up protocol accords in 1996. KEDO signed the supply contract with North Korea in December 1995. With the groundbreaking at the reactor site in August 1997, KEDO official shave changed the estimated completion date from 2003 to 2007; other experts predict a much later date.

KEDO's estimated cost of the reactors in 1994 is currently $4.6 billion. Other estimates have been $5.5-6.0 billion. South Korea is to supply the reactors through a South Korean company as the main contractor; and South Korea and Japan will provide most of the financing. The Administration's objective is to secure all the money for the light water reactors from other governments. It has approached Western European and southeast Asian countries about financial assistance. An Agreement reached by KEDO members on November 9, 1998, sets South Korea's contribution at $3.22 billion, Japan's contribution at $1 billion, and the European Union's contribution at $76 million. This leaves a projected shortfall of $305 million.

The supply contract will add to the financial costs. KEDO accepted several of North Korea's demands for construction of auxiliary facilities: ports, roads, a nuclear waste storage facility, and a reactor simulator. KEDO rejected North Korea's demanded that KEDO finance modernization of North Korea's electric power grid. The cost of this has been estimated at $750 million. North Korea reissued the demand in an amended form in U.S. – North Korean talks in March 2000, calling for U.S. "compensation" for electricity shortages because the light water nuclear reactors will not be completed by 2003.

Clinton Administration officials have noted that before construction begins, the United States, in accord with the Atomic Energy Act, must enter into a bilateral nuclear cooperation agreement with North Korea, since U.S. technology is incorporated into the South Korean light water reactors that North Korea will receive. Administration officials state that light water reactors are less dangerous than North Korea's current graphite reactors, partly because plutonium produced from light water reactors is more technologically difficult to use in the manufacture nuclear weapons. They also assert that North Korea will have to secure enriched uranium fuel for light water reactors from outside North Korea. This, the officials claim, will give the United States leverage on the supply of fuel if North Korea should violate the Agreed Framework. However, non-government nuclear experts assert that North Korea could use the original supply of fuel for the reactors to produce enough plutonium annually for up to 70 atomic bombs before the United States could react by seeking a cutoff of future fuel shipments. Ambassador Gallucci has acknowledged that "a technical possibility" exists that North Korea could use light water reactors to produce plutonium for nuclear weapons. Moreover, exercising U.S. leverage over the supply of fuel would require that potential suppliers of fuel like China and Russia coordinate their policies with the United States. The Agreed Framework and subsequent Clinton Administration have provided no information on the projected costs of supplying the reactor fuel.

Oil at No Cost. Prior to the construction of light water reactors, the Agreed Framework commits the United States to facilitate the provision to North Korea of "alternative energy" to compensate for the freeze of nuclear facilities. The alternative energy is to be "heavy oil". In January 1995, the Clinton Administration arranged for the shipment of 50,000 metric tons of U.S. heavy oil to North Korea. This was followed by a shipment of 100,000 metric tons of oil in October 1995. Starting in October 1996, the United States is to facilitate shipments of 500,000 metric tons of heavy oil to North Korea annually until the first of the two light water reactors becomes operational. The annual cost of the oil currently is over $60 million. The Administration financed the initial shipment of 50,000 tons of oil with $4.5 million from appropriated Defense Department funds designated for "emergency expenses." The European Union joined KEDO's executive board in May 1997 and has provided over $15 million annually for the oil shipments. The Administration has had little success in securing financial support from Southeast Asian and Persian Gulf countries despite repeated requests.

The Agreed Framework states that the heavy oil is "for heating and electricity production." North Korea has only one oil-fired electrical power plant, but 500,000 tons of oil annually exceeds the capacity of this plant. Other potential uses of heavy oil are for ship transport and steel production. U.S. officials disclosed in February 1995 that North Korea had "diverted" a "small amount" of the heavy oil received in January to Industrial uses. Ambassador Gallucci hinted that it was used in steel production. He said that the United States and North Korea had agreed on procedures to ensure against further diversions. However, a General Accounting Office report in late 1999 described periodic breakdowns in the U.S. system of monitoring North Korea's use of the heavy oil. President Clinton notified Congress in March 2000 that he could not certify that North was not diverting heavy oil for unauthorized purposes.

Diplomatic Representation. The United States and North Korea announced in the Agreed Framework an intention to open liaison offices in each other's capital and established full diplomatic relations if the two governments make progress "on issues of concern to each side." By April 1995, most technical arrangements for liaison offices were completed. However, North Korea since has displayed more reluctance to finalize arrangements. Ambassador Gallucci has asserted that a full normalization of diplomatic relations will depend on a successful resolution of non-nuclear military issues, especially the heavy deployment of North Korean conventional military forces along the demilitarized zone separating North and south Korea and North Korea's program to develop and sell to other governments longer range missiles. In October 1999, William Perry, the Administration's Special Adviser on North Korea, cited normalization of diplomatic relations as one of the benefits which the united States could offer North Korea for new agreements on nuclear and missile issues.

Lifting the U.S. Economic Embargo. The Agreed Framework specifies that within three months from October 21, 1994, the two sides will reduce barriers to trade and investment, including restrictions on telecommunications services and financial transactions. This requires the Clinton Administration to relax the U.S. economic embargo on North Korea, which the Truman Administration and Congress put in place during the Korean War. On January 20, 1995, the Administration announced initial measures, including permission for telecommunications links with North Korea, permission for U.S. citizens to use credit cards in north Korea, permission for American media organizations to open offices in north Korea, permission for North Korea to use U.S. banks in financial transactions with third countries, and permission for U.S. steel companies to import magnesite from North Korea. North Korea since has pressed the Clinton Administration to end all economic sanctions. In U.S. – North Korean talks in September 1999, the United States agreed to end a broader range of economic sanctions in exchange for a North Korean moratorium on future missile testing.

KOREA: PROCEDURAL AND JURISDICTIONAL QUESTIONS REGARDING POSSIBLE NORMALIZATION OF RELATIONS WITH NORTH KOREA

Zachary S. David
Larry A. Niksch
Larry Q. Nowels
Vladimir N. Pregelj
Rinn-Sup Shinn
Robert G. Sutter

SUMMARY

The Clinton Administration signed an agreement with North Korea on October 21, 1994, detailing steps to end the crisis caused by North Korea's nuclear program and pledging to "move toward full normalization of political and economic relations." Many details of the accord have not been disclosed, including the precise mechanisms to be used to provide light water nuclear reactors and annual shipments of U.S. heavy oil to North Korea, and a clear process to be followed in normalizing political and economic relations.

As Congress and the Administration consider taking steps to implement the agreement and normalize U.S.-North Korean relations, they will face a complicated array of legal and regulatory restrictions currently governing

U.S.-North Korean relations. These restrictions affect significant aspects of the October 21, accord on nuclear transfers and oil shipments. They cover all areas of official relations including economic, consular, diplomatic, cultural and other interactions. They have often deep historical roots in American opposition to Communist regimes in the cold War and, more specifically, the Korean War.

A review of the legal and regulatory restrictions and an examination of the American experience in normalizing relations with other Communist countries like China and current efforts with Vietnam show that the process of normalization with a Communist country and former military adversary like North Korea could be protracted. Many of the current restrictions on U.S. relations with North Korea are mandated by statutes specifically referring to North Korea or broader statutes affecting certain types of countries that would include North Korea. Some statutes give an element of discretion to the President. Other restrictions on North Korea have been imposed under general statutory or other authorities that have been applied to North Korea by executive decision in response to specific situations or policy goals.

There are a variety of paths that might be followed to normalize relations – e.g., moving ahead first in diplomatic areas while holding back economic ties; moving ahead more quickly in economic than political areas; moving forward in all areas concurrently; etc. In general, the initiative to move ahead rests mainly with the President, but Congress plays an important role in many areas. Without congressional support, full normalization of relations is impossible.

U.S.-NORTH KOREAN RELATIONS SINCE 1948[*]

The United States has no formal relations with the Communist North Korean regime in Pyongyang. North Korea, or the Democratic People's Republic of Korea (DPRK), was established in September 1948 under the aegis of the Soviet Union as a counterweight to South Korea. U.S. policy toward DPRK has since been a function largely of U.S. relations with South Korea; the United States played a direct role in the establishment of the Republic of Korea (R.O.K.) and defended the fragile republic from North Korean aggression in the Korean War (1950-53). In the ensuing decades, the triangular U.S.-North Korean-South Korean relations have been frozen in cold War confrontation. This situation may soon be modified, however, by gradual steps toward normalization of political and economic relations between Washington confrontation. This situation may soon be modified, however, by gradual steps toward normalization of political and economic relations between Washington and Pyongyang. This was made possible under U.S.-North Korean agreements signed in Geneva, in August and October 1994, as part of multilateral effort aimed at "an overall resolution of the nuclear issue on the Korean Peninsula."

U.S. INVOLVEMENT IN KOREA, 1945-1953

Post-war U.S. involvement in Korea began in 1945, when, to effect the surrender of Japanese forces on the Korean Peninsula, the United States and

---

[*] Prepared by Rinn-Sup Shinn, Analyst in Asian Affairs, Foreign Affairs and National Defense Division.

the Soviet Union agreed to divide Korea at the 38th parallel into two military zones of administration. Under the arrangement, Japanese forces surrendered to U.S. forces south—and to Soviet forces north—of that line. Although intended for temporary military expediency, the dividing line became the de facto north-south boundary in 1948, when the two Koreas emerged as rival political entities, both claiming to be the only legitimate government on the peninsular. The United States recognized South Korea; the Soviet Union did the same for North Korea. By December 1948, the Soviet forces had withdrawn from the North and U.S. forces withdrew from the South by the spring of 1949.

THE KOREAN WAR AND THE ARMISTICE AGREEMENT OF 1953

The Korean War was started by Kim IL Sung with backing of Soviet leader Joseph Stalin, a fact confirmed by the recent release of official Soviet documents. The United Nations, in accordance with the terms of its Charter, engaged in its first collective action to repulse the aggressors, established "a unified command for UN Forces in Korea," or the UN Command (UNC), to which 16 member nations sent troops and assistance. With the exception of South Korea, the United States contributed the largest contingent to this UN effort. The battle line seesawed from south to north after large numbers of Chinese "people's volunteers" intervened to save the North from the brink of extinction; by summer 1953, the line had stabilized north of Seoul near the 38th parallel into what is now called the demilitarized zone (DMZ).

Armistice negotiations began in July 1951, but hostilities continued until July 27, 1953, when the military commanders of the North Korean People's Army (KPA), the Chinese "people's volunteers", and the UNC signed an armistice agreement at Panmunjon. Technically, neither the United States nor South Korea is a signatory to the armistice per se, but both continue to adhere to it through the UNC. No comprehensive peace agreement has replaced the armistice. Thus a condition of belligerency still exists on the peninsula. A Military Armistice commission composed of 10 members, five appointed by either side, was to supervise implementation of the pact. The war claimed the lives of 54,540 American servicemen (including 33,870 in combat) and left 103,284 wounded and some 7,900 Americans still unaccounted for. (Beginning in May 1990, North Korea handed over 208 sets of "remains" claimed to be those of Americans; in 1993, the U.S.

Defense Department paid $890,000 to Pyongyang for 46 of these returned sets in compensation for itemized "expenses"; the U.S. side wants to limit compensation to $2,000 to $3,000 per set of remains, while the North reportedly demands $30,000 each.) Korean casualties, North and South, numbered in the millions. (North Korea remains silent to human toll to this day.)

The armistice called for a political resolution to the problem of Korea's division within three months. An international political conference met in Geneva in April 1954 but, after seven weeks of futile Cold War-influenced debate, ended without agreement or progress.

ARMED CONFRONTATION, 1953-1980S

For nearly four decades since the end of the Korean War, the United States has not had a specific policy directed toward North Korea. In fact, whatever policy it did have was aimed largely at complementing its policy toward south Korea, ensuring the security of the south, and maintaining close bilateral ties. Tot hat end, the United States has maintained a military presence in the south under the 1954 Mutual Defense Treaty. For its part, North Korea concluded mutual security treaties with the Soviet Union and china in 1961 and has continued to build up its military strength as part of its continuing – and economically draining – effort to counter U.S./R.O.K. forces in the South.

Through the 1980s and beyond, the United States continued to face a hostile North Korea under Kim Il-Sung, who tried a mix of soft and hard-line approaches toward Washington. In the 1960s, the United States had to contend with belligerent North Korean actions such as the 1968 seizure of U.S.S. Pueblo near Wonsan and the 1969 downing of a U.S. reconnaissance plane off Chongjin.

In the 1970s, U.S.-North Korean relations remained frigid, despite Pyongyang's assertions that the historic beginning of inter-Korean dialogue in 1972 opened a new era of peace on the peninsular. North Korea contended that the United States should withdraw its troops from the South, since the two Koreas had agreed in July 1972 to cooperate for peace and unification. It also began to signal its desire for people-to-people contacts in direct appeals to the United States. In march 1974, in a letter addressed to the United States Congress, North Korea proposed bilateral negotiations on replacing the "outdated" Korean armistice with "a peace agreement." It argued that direct talks were necessary inasmuch as the United States, not

South Korea, had the real power of command and control over South Korean security. Also on Pyongyang's agenda was the demand that U.S. troops to be withdrawn from the south as early as possible. In 1975, North Korea began to complain that U.S. nuclear arsenals in the south posed a new threat to the DPRK.

Then, as now, the U.S. policy was to encourage dialogue between the two Koreas for mutual accommodations and to ensure peace and stability on the peninsula. Toward the end of 1974, the United States signaled to the Soviet Union and China its willingness to improve relations with North Korea, provided that Moscow and Beijing would take similar steps toward South Korea. In January 1975, North Korea criticized the so-called "cross-recognition" formula as a plot to perpetuate the division of Korea. In a message intended for the two communist allies, Pyongyang pointedly noted that "a socialist country by nature cannot deal with the puppets raised by the imperialists, much less 'recognize' them." Otherwise, Pyongyang insisted, "it would be tantamount to recognizing the U.S. imperialist occupation of South Korea."

In the mid-1970s, the United States heightened its vigilance against North Korea, after the discovery in late 1974 of a North Korean tunnel dug under the demilitarized zone (a second tunnel was uncovered in February 1975). Shortly before the fall of Saigon in April 1975, there were also troubling reports out of Beijing that Chinese officials had cautioned Kim Il tunnel dug under the demilitarized zone (a second tunnel was uncovered in February 1975). Shortly before the fall of Saigon in April 1975, there were also troubling reports out of Beijing that Chinese officials had cautioned Kim Il Sung, at the time of his Sudden visit to Beijing on April 18, against launching an attack on south Korea. Then in August 1976, there were North Korean axe murders of two American officers attached to the UNC at Panmunjon. Against this backdrop, the first of U.S.-R.O.K. "Team Spirit" joint military exercises began in 1976.

Under the Carter Administration (1977-80), U.S. policy toward North/South Korea took a new turn. In March 1977, President Carter announced his intention to pull out all of the 40,000 .S. ground forces in the South during the next four to five years, adding that "I am very determined to take this action." Also announced was his intention to lift restrictions on travel by U.S. citizens to North Korea, Cuba, Vietnam, and Cambodia on March 18, 1977, on the ground that these restrictions violated human rights. Two years later, in July at the end of his state visit to Seoul, Carter and his South Korean counterpart jointly proposed to North Korea a tripartite conference for the resolution of Korean problems. Pyongyang rejected it in the belief that an acceptance would amount to tacit recognition of South Korea – and by implication an acknowledgment of a two-Korea policy that North Korea claimed was being pursued by Washington. Later in July 1979, however, Carter ordered a halt to the withdrawal of the remaining 32,000 U.S. combat troops, the "timing and pace" of any further troop reduction was to be reexamined in two years.

Under the Reagan Administration (1981-1988), U.S. relations with North Korea showed no sign of movement, even though the Administration in November 1983 urged Pyongyang to come to a tripartite conference; in January 1984, North Korea proposed a similar meeting to be convened on its own terms. But circumstances then were not conducive to dialogue. In early 1985, North Korea had launched an ultra-nationalistic, anti-America propaganda offensive designed to create social and political unrest in the south. This was designed to capitalize on the groundswell of anti-American sentiments among South Koreans in the wake of a civil uprising in Kwangju in 1980, suppressed in a bloody crackdown by U.S.-backed South Korean troops. Pyongyang sought to incite South Korean students and dissidents to anti-American actions, blaming the United States for the continuing territorial division and the resulting "agony and misery of the Korean people." Through clandestine publications (the quarterly Ch'ongmaek in particular) and the Voice of National Salvation broadcasts, North Korea urged south Koreans of all walks to rise up in "anti-U.S., pro-independence" struggles. To that end, Pyongyang in August 1985 inaugurated an anti-U.S./anti-R.O.K. underground organization called the "South Korean National Democratic Front" – actually a renaming of the North Korea-based "reunification and Revolutionary Party" at the disposal of Pyongyang since 1969, as an instrument of propaganda, agitation, and misinformation against U.S./R.O.K. interests.

Other factors hampering U.S.-North Korean relations included the October 1983 assassination attempt on the South Korean President Chun Doo Hwan in Rangoon, Burma. Although Chun was not harmed, 17 members of his south Korean entourage, as well as four Burmese officials, were killed by a bomb planted by North Korean agents. Then, in November 1987, in an attempt to underscore Pyongyang's assertions that Seoul would be a highly unsafe place to go for the 1988 summer Olympics, agents of North Korea on order from top leadership sabotaged a Korean Airlines plane over the Indian Ocean, causing the deaths of all 115 passengers on board. Since January 1988, North Korea has been on the U.S. Government list of states supporting international terrorism. North Korea is also subject to a general embargo on trade and financial transactions under the Trading with the Enemy Act.

CONFRONTATION WITH LIMITED BILATERAL CONTACTS, 1988-91

Shortly before the Seoul Olympics (September 17-October 2, 1988), the United States indicated to North Korea that it would move toward improving relations if North Korea did not disrupt the Summer Olympics. At the end of October 1988, the U.S. announced a package of steps on relations with the North. This initiative was also in support of South Korean Presidential Roh Tae Woo's July 7, 1988 overture aimed at drawing Pyongyang out of its isolation, promoting free inter-Korean cross-border movement of people and goods, and cooperating an international forums. The modest package authorized U.S. diplomats to hold substantive discussions with North Korean counterparts in neutral settings; encourage unofficial, nongovernmental visits from North Korea for academic and cultural purposes; facilitate the travel of U.S. citizens to North Korea for family visits, academic and cultural purposes and so on; and permit humanitarian trade in items meeting "basic human needs," on a case-by-case basis.

Beginning in December 1988, the U.S. Embassy's political counselor in Beijing met with his North Korean counterpart 33 times, most recently in May 1993. In these meetings, the United States suggested several issue areas in which North Korea could take positive steps as part of a sustained, reciprocal process. These areas included:

- Progress in dialogue with South Korea, including serious discussion with the South about confidence-building measures and other concrete steps to reduce tensions;

- Conclusion and implementation of an International Atomic Energy Agency (IAEA) safeguards agreement, as required under the Nuclear Nonproliferation Treaty (NPT);

- Regularization of a process for returning Korean War remains of U.S. servicemen missing in action (MIAs) and an eventual accounting for all MIAs from the Korean War;

- A credible statement condemning terrorism; and
- Demonstration of greater respect for human rights.

The United States also expressed its concern about North Korean exports of ballistic missiles and related military technology.

For its part, North Korea repeated its demand for replacing the 1953 armistice with a peace treaty, withdrawal of U.S. troops from the South, and upgrading the status of talks in Beijing. The United States recognizes that the future of Korean issues is a matter for the authorities of North and South Korea to resolve peacefully through negotiations. As the fundamental decisions must be made by the Korean people themselves, the United States refuses to be drawn into separate negotiations with North Korea on the 1953 armistice. The United States remains prepared, however, to participate in talks with the representatives of North and South Korea, if so desired by the two Korean governments, provided that both are full and equal participants in any such talks.

THE NUCLEAR ISSUE IN U.S.-NORTH KOREAN RELATIONS, 1992-94

In the early 1990s, Pyongyang's suspected nuclear weapons program overshadowed all other issues in U.S.-North Korean relations. The United States and other countries sought North Korean adherence to its obligations as a signatory to the NPT since 1985. As inducements, U.S. nuclear warheads were withdrawn from South Korea in late 1991, followed by South Korean President Roh's announcement that there were no nuclear arms in the South. Additionally, the United States and South Korea offered to cancel the 1992 Team Spirit joint military exercise, which Pyongyang had long criticized as rehearsals for nuclear attack against the North; and in January 1992, in New York, U.S. Undersecretary of State Arnold Kanter had a first high-level meeting with North Korea's Kim Yong Sun, the ruling Korean Workers party secretary for international affairs. At the meeting, both sides outlined their respective policies on bilateral and inter-Korean issues -- the

U.S. side especially underscoring the critical important of North Korea's nuclear transparency.

At the end of January 1992, North Korea signed a NPT safeguards agreement after six years of stonewalling, and the following month, North and South Korea exchanged signed texts of a Joint Declaration on the Denuclearization of the Korean Peninsula that they had initialed in December 1991. From June 1992 to February 1993, the IAEA was allowed to conduct six regular inspections of North Korea's seven declared nuclear facilities. Meanwhile, inter-Korean negotiations over the implementation of the North/South denuclearization accord were broken off by North Korea, which argued that the nuclear issue should be resolved only through bilateral talks with Washington, not with South Korea or the IAEA.

By late 1992, IAEA inspectors found evidence suggesting that North Korea had reprocessed more plutonium than it had declared to the IAEA; plutonium is a key ingredient in the making of nuclear bombs. Rejecting the IAEA demand for special inspections of two nuclear waste sites at Yongbyon that could reveal the history of reprocessing dating back to 1989, Pyongyang announced its decision to withdraw from the NPT on March 12, 1993. It contended that the IAEA violated the principle of "impartiality" as it had relied on intelligence provided by "a third country" (the United States) in calling for special inspections. Pyongyang asserted that such intrusive inspections were part of a U.S. plot to undo North Korea. In May 1993, the United Nations Security Council passed a resolution, urging the North to cooperate with the IAEA and to implement the inter-Korean denuclearization accord. It also called on all member states to encourage North Korea to respond positively to the resolution and to facilitate a solution.

To persuade North Korea to return to the NPT, the Clinton Administration held talks with North Korea in early June 1993, in New York, that led to North Korea "suspending" its withdrawal from the NPT on June 11. A second round of talks was held by July, in Geneva, to set the guidelines for resolving the nuclear issue, inter alia, by exploring ways in which new light water reactors, not capable of producing nuclear weapons material, could be provided to North Korea, for laying the basis for improving overall U.S.-North Korean relations, and for restarting inter-Korean dialogue.

In 1994, however, the crisis surged as North Korea not only continued to reject an IAEA full-scope inspection but, in May, removed 8,000 fuel rods from its 25-megawatt reactor, without permitting monitoring by IAEA inspectors. The Clinton Administration began to discuss possible UN sanctions against the North. Pyongyang responded by announcing its intent to withdraw from the IAEA. The mounting crisis was defused, however, after former President Jimmy Carter held talks in June, in Pyongyang, with Kim Il Sung. As a result, a third round of U.S.-North Korean talks opened in Geneva on July 8, 1994, but was cut short by Kim Il Sung's death. An historic North-South Korean summit meeting, planned for late July, was put off indefinitely.

AGREED STATEMENT OF AUGUST 12, 1994

Resumed in Geneva on August 5, 1994, the talks produced an "agreed statement" of August 12. The joint statement stated that the following "elements" should be part of a final resolution of the nuclear issue.

- North Korea is prepared to replace its graphite-moderated reactors with light water reactors (LWRs); the United States is prepared to make arrangements or the provision of LWRs of about 2,000 megawatts total to the North and to make arrangements for the supply of interim energy alternatives pending the transfer of the LWRs.

- Once the United States provides the assurances for the provision of the LWRs and interim energy alternatives, North Korea will freeze construction of 50- and 200-megawatt graphite-moderated reactors now under construction, forego reprocessing 8,000 spent fuel rods placed in a cooling pond, and seal its reprocessing facility called "radiochemical laboratory," to be monitored by the IAEA.

- The United States is prepared to provide North Korea with assurances against the threat or use of nuclear weapons; to agree to establishment of diplomatic representation in each other's capitals; and to reduce barriers to trade and investment as a move toward full normalization of political and economic relations with North Korea.

- In return, North Korea is prepared to remain a party to the NPT, to allow implementation of its NPT safeguards agreement and to implement the North-South [Korean] Joint Declaration on the Denuclearization of the Korean Peninsula.

Both sides also agreed that important issues raised during the talks remained to be resolved, that expert-level discussions were need to hammer out technical details of the agreed statement, and that U.S.-North Korean talks would resume in Geneva on September 23, 1994.

AGREED FRAMEWORK OF OCTOBER 21, 1994

After 17 months of difficult on-and-off negotiations, the two countries signed an "agreed framework" in Geneva, on October 21, 1994, paving the way for ending their nuclear dispute and for moving toward improving their relations (For particulars, see Appendix I. The Agreed Framework between the United States and the Democratic People's Republic of Korea, October 21, 1994). The agreement has a confidential annex detailing how the agreement will be put into effect.

The agreed framework is consistent with the broad elements of the August 12 agreed statement. Under the accord, North Korea is to freeze its nuclear activities and "eventually" dismantle its nuclear facilities by the time the second internationally supplied reactor is completed; open two nuclear waste sites to IAEA inspections "when a significant portion of the light water reactor project is completed, but before delivery of key nuclear components." The two sides also agreed to hold expert talks to discuss arrangements for spent fuel storage and ultimate disposition of 8,000 fuel rods unloaded in May 1994 from the existing 25-megawatt thermal (5-megawatt electrical) reactor. The spent fuel is to be shipped out of North Korea by the time the first reactor is completed.

In exchange, North Korea will be provided electrical with two new LWRs with a combined generating capacity of around 2,000 megawatts by a target date of 2003. To compensate the North for not restarting the 25-megawatt reactor and for halting construction of 50- and 200-megawatt reactors, North Korea will receive 500,000 metric tons of free heavy oil annually as an interim energy source for heating and generation of electricity until the light water reactor project is finished.

The United States also pledged to set up an international consortium (tentatively called the Korea Energy Development Organization – KDO) to finance and undertake the light water reactor project worth about $4 billion; South Korea will reportedly pay for around 55 percent of the total, with Japan and others paying the balance. Consortium participants include South Korea, Japan and several other countries. In his October 20, 1994, letter addressed to "Kim Jong Il, Supreme Leader" of the DPRK, President Clinton confirmed that he would "use the full powers of my office to facilitate arrangements" for the light water project and for "the funding and implementation of interim energy alternatives" pending completion of the first reactor unit of the project. In the event of some unforeseen difficulties in completing the deal, Clinton assured that the United States would itself, "to the extent necessary," honor the accord, "subject to approval of the U.S. Congress" (see Appendix II. President Clinton's Letter of Assurance to Kim Jong Il, October 20, 1994).

The October deal also contains a North Korean pledge to "engage in North-South dialogue, as this Agreed Framework will help create an atmosphere that promotes such dialogue." The outcome of such dialogue, always contentious in the past, will have a significant bearing on how the Agreed Framework will be implemented, since South Korea is to play a key role in providing light water reactors – a role Pyongyang seems to have condoned reluctantly.

APPENDIX I

The Agreed Framework between the United States and the Democratic People's Republic of Korea
Geneva, October 21, 1994

Delegations of the Governments of the United States of America (U.S.) and the Democratic People's Republic of Korea (DPRK) held talks in Geneva from September 23 to October 17, 1994, to negotiate an overall resolution of the nuclear issue on the Korean Peninsula.

Both sides reaffirmed the importance of attaining the objectives contained in the August 12, 1994 Agreed Statement between the U.S. and the DPRK and upholding the principles of the June 11, 1993 Joint Statement of the U.S. and the DPRK to achieve peace and security on a nuclear-free Korean peninsula. The U.S. and the DPRK decided to take the following actions for the resolution of the nuclear issue:

I. Both sides will cooperate to replace the DPRK's graphite-moderated reactors and related facilities with light-water reactor (LWR) power plants.

   1) In accordance with the October 20, 1994 letter of assurance from the U.S. President, the U.S. will undertake to make arrangements for the provision to the DPRK of a LWR project with a total generating capacity of approximately 2,000 MW(e) by a target date of 2003.

   – The U.S. will organize under its leadership an international consortium to finance and supply contract with the DPRX within six months of the date of this Document for the provision of the LWR project. Contract talks will begin as soon as possible after the date of this Document.

   – The U.S., representing the consortium, will make best efforts to secure the conclusions, of a supply contract with the DPRK within six months of the date of this Document for the provision of the LWR project. Contract talks will begin as soon as possible after the date of this Document.

2) In accordance with the October 20, 1994 letter of assurance from the U.S. President, the U.S., representing the consortium, will make arrangements to offset the energy foregone due to the freeze of the DPRK's graphite-moderated reactors and related facilities, pending completion of the first LWR unit.

— Alternative energy will be provided in the form of heavy oil for heating and electricity production.

— Deliveries of heavy oil will begin within three months of the date of this Document and will reach a rate of 500,000 tons annually, in accordance with an agreed schedule of deliveries.

3) Upon receipt of U.S. assurances for the provision of LWR's and for arrangements for interim energy alternatives, the DPRK will freeze its graphite-moderated reactors and related facilities.

— The freeze on the DPRK's graphite-moderated reactors and related facilities will be fully implemented within one month of the date of this Document. During this one-month period, and throughout the freeze, the International Atomic Energy Agency (IAEA) will be allowed to monitor this freeze, and the DPRK will provide full cooperation to the IAEA for this purpose.

— Dismantlement of the DPRK's graphite-moderated reactors and related facilities will be completed when the LWR project is completed.

— The U.S. and DPRK will cooperated in finding a method to store safely the spent fuel from the 5 MW(e) experimental reactor during the construction of the LWR project, and to dispose to the fuel in a safe manner that does not involve reprocessing in the DPRK.

4) As soon as possible after the date of this document. U.S. and DPRK experts will hold two sets of experts talks.

- At one set of talks, experts all discuss issues related to alternative energy and the replacement of the graphite-moderated reactor program with the LWR project.

- At the other set of talks, experts will discuss specific arrangements for spent fuel storage and ultimate disposition.

II. The two sides will move toward full normalization of political and economic relations.

1) Within three months of the date of this Document, both sides will reduce barriers to trade and investment, including restrictions on telecommunications services and financial transactions.

2) Each side will open a liaison office in the other's capital following resolution of consular and other technical issues through expert level discussions.

3) As progress is made on issues of concern to each side, the U.S. and DPRK will upgrade bilateral relations to the Ambassadorial level.

III. Both sides will work together for peace and security on a nuclear-free Korean peninsula.

1) The U.S. will provide formal assurances to the DPRK, against the threat or use of nuclear weapons by the U.S.

2) The DPRK will consistently take steps to implement the North-South Joint Declaration on the Denuclearization of the Korean peninsula.

3) The DPRK will engage in North-South dialogue, as this Agreed Framework will help create an atmosphere that promotes such dialogue.

IV. Both sides will work together to strengthen the international nuclear non-proliferation regime.

1) The DPRK will remain a party to the Treaty on the Non-Proliferation of Nuclear Weapons (NPT) and will allow implementation of its safeguards agreement unde the Treaty.

2) Upon conclusion of the supply contract for the provision of the LWR project, ad hoc and routine inspections will resume under the DPRK's safeguards agreement with the IAEA with respect to the facilities not subject to the freeze. Pending conclusion of the supply contract, inspections required by the IAEA for the continuity of safeguards will continue at the facilities not subject to the freeze.

3) When a significant portion of the LWR project is completed, but before delivery of key nuclear components, the DPRK will come into full compliance with its safeguards agreement with the IAEA (INFCIRC/403), including taking all steps that may be deemed necessary by the IAEA, following consultations with the Agency with regard to verifying the accuracy and completeness of the DPRK's initial report on all nuclear material in the DPRK.

Kang Sok Ju – Head of the Delegation for the Democratic People's Republic of Korea, First Vice-Minister of Foreign Affairs of the Democratic People's Republic of Korea

Robert L. Gallucci – Head of the Delegation of United States of America, Ambassador at Large of the United States of America.

Source: U.S. Department of State

APPENDIX II

President Clinton's Letter to Kim Jong Il

The White House
Washington

October 20, 1994

Excellency:

    I wish to confirm to you that I will use the full powers of my office to facilitate arrangements for the financing and construction of a light-water nuclear power reactor project within the DPRK, and the funding and implementation of interim energy alternatives for the Democratic People's Republic of Korea pending completion of the first reactor unit of the light-water reactor project. In addition, in the event that this reactor project is not completed for reasons beyond the control of the DPRK, I will use the full powers of my office to provide, to the extent necessary, such a project from the United States, subject to approval of the U.S. Congress. Similarly, in the event that the interim energy alternatives are not provided for reasons beyond the control of the DPRK, I will use the full powers of my office to provide, to the extent necessary, such interim energy alternatives from the United States, subject to the approval of the U.S. Congress.

    I will follow this course of action so long as the DPRK continues to implement the policies described in the Agreed Framework Between the United States of America and the Democratic People's Republic of Korea.

    Sincerely,

Bill Clinton

His Excellency Kim Jong Il
Supreme Leader of the Democratic
People's Republic of Korea
Pyongyang

WHAT IS THE CURRENT STATUS OF U.S.-NORTH KOREAN POLITICAL RELATIONS?*

The United States does not have normal diplomatic relations with the North Korean government. It maintains no diplomatic, consular or trade relations with authorities there.

The United States has recognized the Democratic Peoples Republic of Korea as a state in the international law sense. Moreover, the United States has acknowledged that the government of the DPRK exercises effective control within North Korea. In recent years, U.S. officials have dealt with DPRK authorities on a range of issues centered on North Korea's nuclear program. In addition, a few members of Congress have traveled to North Korea for talks with DPRK officials.

The United States recognizes that the future of the Korean peninsula is primarily a matter for the people of Korea to decide. The U.S. Government believes that a constructive dialogue between the authorities of south and North Korea to resolve the issues on the peninsula, and that concrete steps to promote greater understanding and reduce tension, are needed to pave the way for unifying the Korean nation. Because the fundamental decision must be taken by the Korean people themselves, the United States refuses to be drawn into separate negotiations with North Korea, as Pyongyang has insisted, on replacing the 1953 armistice with a peace treaty. The United States remains prepared to participate in negotiations between representatives of North and South Korea, if so desired by the two Korean governments and provided that both are full and equal participants in such talks.

---

* Prepared by Robert G. Sutter, Senior Specialist in International Policies.

WHICH BRANCH OF THE U.S. GOVERNMENT HAS RESPONSIBILITY FOR NORMALIZING POLITICAL RELATIONS?

The Constitution divides the foreign relations powers between the executive and legislative branches of the government. For example, the Constitution gives the President the power to send and receive ambassadors, while Congress has the power to regulate commerce with foreign nations, to defined offenses against the law of nations, and to declare war. The President and the Senate share the power to make treaties and appoint ambassadors.

Although the Constitution does not ascribe the powers of recognizing states and governments to any particular branch of the Government, the President traditionally exercises such authority. The legislative branch of the Government exercises little direct influence over the normalization of relations. Congress, however, controls appropriations that are necessary to implement the President's plan to establish relations.

WHAT ARE THE DIFFERENCE PROCESSES INVOLVED IN ESTABLISHING GOVERNMENT-TO-GOVERNMENT RELATIONS?

General aspects of the process of establishing relations between governments include: 1) recognition of a sovereign state, and 2) establishment of diplomatic relations. Governments can choose to recognize a state – such recognition is accorded to an entity having a defined area and population under the control of a government that has the capacity to engage in foreign relations. Recognition of a state, however, does not necessarily mean that a government may recognize the government of that state. Often times, political considerations influence a government's willingness to establish or reestablish diplomatic relations with the foreign state.

WHAT ARE THE PROCEDURES TO ESTABLISH AN INTEREST SECTION? A LIAISON OFFICE?

In certain cases, the United States has maintained interest sections or liaison offices in countries with which it has no diplomatic relations. In the case of Cuba, for instance, the United States conducts business with Cuba through the U.S. Interests Section in Havana. The Interests Section is officially part of the Swiss Embassy, but is located in the former U.S. Embassy building. The Cuban Interests Section in Washington operates through the Swiss Embassy, although it is located in the former Cuban Embassy building. The State Department was responsible for negotiating the agreement with the Government of Cuba that led to the creation of the respective interests sections.

The United States maintained a liaison office in Bejing from 1973 until it established diplomatic relations with the People's Republic of China (PRC) in 1979. Until 1979, the United States officially had relations with the government of the Republic of China – located in Taiwan. Upon establishing diplomatic relations with the PRC in 1979, the United States broke official relations with Taiwan.

Currently, American commercial and cultural interaction with the people of Taiwan is facilitated through the American Institute in Taiwan (AIT) – a nongovernmental entity staffed largely by U.S. State Department and other officials who are temporarily separated from the U.S. State Department and other officials who are temporarily separated from the U.S. Government. The AIT was established under the authority of the Taiwan Relations Act (P.L. 96-8, 22 U.S.C. 3301-3316). Section 7(A) of the Act authorizes personnel at the AIT to perform notarial, conservator, and consular services. Section 10(c) of the Act provides the means to grant diplomatic privileges and immunities to the Coordination Council for North American Affairs (the Taiwanese Liaison office in Washington, now known as the "Taipei Economic and Cultural Representative Office"), and to its personnel.

In 1994, the United States announced that it would soon exchange liaison offices with Vietnam. While the U.S. passed legislation to allow for establishing liaison offices with China, such legislation was said not to be needed in the case of liaison offices with Vietnam as both Vietnam and the U.S. are parties to multilateral conventions governing diplomatic and consular relations. Later in 1994, the Clinton Administration expressed a willingness to consider opening liaison offices with North Korea. Since

North Korea is also a party to the multilateral conventions, U.S. legislation is seen as not needed in the case of a U.S. liaison office with North Korea.

IF THE UNITED STATES WERE TO NORMALIZE DIPLOMATIC RELATIONS WITH NORTH KOREA, WHAT FURTHER STEPS MIGHT THE UNITED STATES CONSIDER TAKING?

Cultural and Educational Exchanges

The United States has no official cultural, scientific, or educational exchange programs with North Korea. If the United States were interested in pursuing such programs with North Korea it might look to the U.S.-Chinese experience as a model.

In January 1979, the United States and China signed a Cultural Agreement that has established a long-term basis for official exchanges. According to the agreement, the U.S. Information Agency is charged with managing the U.S.-China cultural exchange program. The agreement, however, governs only official, government-to-government contacts, and neither precludes nor covers U.S.-China cultural exchanges that may be privately sponsored. As has occurred under any official U.S.-China agreements, costs of the official cultural exchange programs have been arranged, with each country covering the costs of its own involvement.

Travel Restrictions

The United States has no restrictions against U.S. citizens travelling to North Korea. Freedom of travel is limited in part by strict restrictions on the amount of money and the use of credit cards and other financial instruments by U.S. citizens in North Korea, governed by the Office of Foreign Assets Control of the U.S. Treasury (see section on U.S.-North Korean commercial relations). Because the United States has no consular establishment in North Korea at this time, the State Department is able to provide no assistance to U.S. citizens travelling there.

Consular Agreement

The United States and North Korea may decide to conclude a consular agreement. Since both sides are parties to multilateral conventions governing consular relations, such an agreement may appear redundant. Nevertheless, supporters of such bilateral consular agreements see them as possibly increasing the ability of U.S. diplomats to visit promptly Americans imprisoned abroad. If a bilateral consular treaty is reached, as it was the China in 1981, it would require congressional approval.

U.S.-NORTH KOREAN MILITARY RELATIONS*

U.S. military relations with North Korea are governed by: the armistice of 1953 which ended the Korean War; the role of U.S. troops in south Korea (currently about 36,000) to help defend against a North Korean attack; and the Mutual Defense Treaty between the United States and South Korea, signed in 1953 and ratified in 1954. North Korea has proposed negotiating with the United States (without South Korea's participation) for the replacement of the armistice with a U.S.-North Korean peace agreement. According to North Korea's proposal, first made in 1974, a peace agreement would provide for the withdrawal American forces from South Korea.

Proposals of changes in the armistice agreement, the size and operations of U.S. troops, and in the U.S.-R.O.K. (Republic of Korea) Mutual Defense Treaty would constitute major policy questions for the Clinton Administration and Congress. They also involve several legal and technical issues, some of which overlap with policy questions.

Several technical and possibly financial issues in any U.S. troop withdrawal would involve provisions in the U.S.-R.O.K. status of forces agreement. Signed in 1966 and entered into force in 1967, the U.S-R.O.K. Status of Forces Agreement stipulates rights, obligations, and understandings between the two governments regarding base facilities, entry and exit of Us. Military personnel, customs duties, and criminal jurisdiction necessary for the stationing of U.S. forces in Korea.

---

* Prepared by Larry A. Niksch, Senior Specialist in Asian Affairs.

THE ARMISTICE AGREEMENT

The Korean armistice agreement was signed on July 27, 1953, by military representatives of the United Nations Command, North Korea, and China. The agreement set up an armistice commission composed of the three signatories. The United Nations Command was established by a UN Security Council resolution of July 7, 1950. The resolution placed a "unified command ... under the United States." The command was authorized "at its discretion to use the United Nations flag." The resolution gave the United States broad authority, requiring it only to report to the Security Council "as appropriate."

From July 1953 to the present, the UN Commander in Korea has been the American general who commands U.S. forces in South Korea. Until 1979, the UN Commander had operational command of U.S. and R.O.K. Combined Forces Command.[27] This left the UN command with responsibility for only the armistice, participating in the armistice commission and administering the Joint Security Area in Panmunjon, where the commission meets.

Moreover, the makeup and operation of the armistice commission has changed since 1990. Under a U.S.-R.O.K. agreement in March 1991, a South Korean general replaced an American general as head of the UN tea on the armistice commission. In 1953, South Korea had refused to sign the armistice and had not participated in the armistice commission. North Korea refused to meet with the new South Korea-led team and announced n April 1994 that it was withdrawing from the commission.[28] China made a similar withdrawal announcement in early September 1994.

The U.S. Government, through the UN Commander in Korea, would have wide prerogative in negotiating changes in the armistice agreement or even negotiating a new armistice accord. If the U.S. Government directly negotiated a peace agreement with North Korea that replaced the armistice agreement, the UN Security Council or the General Assembly probably would consider action to abolish the UN Command. In 1975, under the Ford Administration, the United States submitted a resolution of the General Assembly to disband the UN Command if alternative arrangements to

---

[27] Pollack, Samuel. Self Doubts on Approaching Forth: The United Nations' Oldest and Only Collective Security Enforcement Army, the United Nations Command in Korea. In *Dickinson Journal of International Law*, Vol. 6, No. 1. P. 16.

[28] Radio Pyongyang, April 28, 1994. Text of North Korean Foreign Ministry Statement.

maintain the armistice were found.[29] With regard to the role of Congress, the Clinton Administration might argue that since Congress did not declare war during the Korean conflict, it would not have to ratify a peace agreement.

If South Korea did not participate in U.S.-North Korean negotiations, South Korea presumably would not be bound legally by such an accord. However, South Korea's participation in the Combined Forces command (CFC) would constitute a means by which the United States could ensure South Korean compliance, if the commander of the CFC were given responsibility for administering provisions of a peace agreement similar to provisions of the armistice agreement (for example, the status of the demilitarized zone and investigations and negotiations of violations of the agreement). The CFC commander would need operational control over R.O.K. forces related to such provisions. Gaining this kind of command authority provably would require U.S.-R.O.K. negotiations and amendments to agreements governing the CFC.

Such procedural problems could be avoided partially if South Korea were included in negotiations over a peace agreement. South Korea would then be a full party to any agreement. However, the inclusion of South Korea in any such negotiation is a policy issue in large part because of North Korea's opposition to inclusion of South Korea in talks over a peace accord.

WITHDRAWING U.S. TROOPS; ENDING THE U.S.-R.O.K. MUTUAL DEFENSE TREATY

The U.S.-R.O.K. Mutual Defense Treaty contains the following language: "Either Party may terminate it [the treaty] one year after notice has been given to the other Party." Under identical language, the United States gave Taiwan a one year's notice in 1979 for termination of the U.S. Republic of China Mutual Defense Treaty.

The Carter Administration invoked the treaty's one year's notice despite a sense-of-Congress resolution passed in 1978 as part of the FY 1979 foreign assistance act. That resolution stated that there should be "prior consultation between Congress and the executive branch on any proposed policy changes affecting the continuation in force of the Mutual Defense Treaty of 1954." Following the Carter Administration's announcement of the one year's

---

[29] Pollack, p. 18.

notice, the Senate passed a "sense of the Senate" resolution declaring that Senate approval "is required to terminate any mutual defense treaty between the United States and another nation." Senator Barry Goldwater also filed the suit in federal court seeking to block the treaty's abrogation without Senate approval. A federal district judge ruled in Goldwater's favor, but the appeals court overturned that decision. The appeals court, however noted special circumstances regarding the treaty with Taiwan and said that the ruling applied only to that treaty.[30]

A U.S. decision to withdraw U.S. troops from South Korea would not be prohibited by the Mutual Defense Treaty or any other U.S.-R.O.K. agreement. The Bush Administration unilaterally withdrew about 7,000 troops from South Korea during the 1990-1992 period without legal impediments.[31] The United States progressively reduced the number of its troops in South Korea from the end of the Korean War until the mid-1970s. The Carter Administration abandoned its plan to withdraw American ground forces because of policy reasons, not legal restrictions.

The Carter Administration came under heavy criticism from both the House and Senate over the withdrawal policy (a key reason for Carter's cancellation of the withdrawal), but Congress made no legislative attempt to mandate a retention of ground troops in South Korea.[32]

Nevertheless, the United States and South Korea have set up a security consultative system, composed of several organizations that undoubtedly would be utilized to discuss issues related to a U.S. decision to withdraw. An annual R.O.K.-U.S. Security Consultative Meeting at the defense ministers' level no doubt would consider policy questions as well as broad procedural issues. These might include: the scheduling of withdrawals, the status of base infrastructure, allowances for Korean workers at U.S. bases, and disbandment of joint U.S.-R.O.K. command organizations, including the Combined Forces Command. Much of the detailed drafting of procedural arrangements would be carried out by the Policy Review Subcommittee and the Logistics Cooperation Committee. The U.S.-R.O.K. commands also establish other working level groups as the need arises. One could expect

---

[30] Congressional Quarterly, Inc. China: U.S. Policy Since 1945. Washington, D.C., 1980. P. 39-42.
[31] U.S. Department of Defense. A Strategic Framework for the Asian Pacific Rim. Report to Congress, 1992, pp. 19-20.
[32] Niksch, Larry A. U.S. Troop Withdrawal from South Korea: Past Shortcomings and Future Prospects. Asian Survey, March 1981. P. 325-341.

that they would set up a number of these groups to draft specific plans for a troop withdrawal.[33] Under the U.S.-R.O.K. Status of Forces Agreement (SOFA), a joint committee sets policies and procedures related to Korean workers at U.S. bases.[34]

---

[33] For a description of the security consultation system, see: R.O.K. Ministry of Defense. Defense White paper, 1991-1992. Pp. 157-161.
[34] R.O.K. Ministry of Defense. Defense White Paper, 1993-1994. P. 115.

NORMALIZING U.S. COMMERCIAL RELATIONS WITH NORTH KOREA[*]

This section discusses restrictions at present in force on U.S. commercial relations with North Korea, and presents a brief history, and the means for their removal or modification. Some changes in the restrictions are likely to be made in the short term pursuant to the recent U.S.-North Korea framework agreement on North Korean nuclear issues.

BACKGROUND

For well over four decades – longer than any other country – North Korea has been the target of a regime of U.S. commercial sanctions of the most comprehensive and restrictive kind. Because of their varied rationale and historical development, these sanctions also at times overlap and are duplicative. In additional to – and along with – a virtually total embargo on U.S. commercial and financial transactions and blocking of North Korean assets in the United States, imposed in 1950, various other types of transactions (specific aspects of merchandise trade, export credits, private investments) are prohibited, limited, or subject to discriminatory practices.

Apart from the sanctions imposed unilaterally by the United States, economic relations between the United States and North Korea are adversely affected by North Korea's reluctance to engage in broad international economic relations. Example include North Korea's nonparticipation in various international economic entities and compacts (e.g., the International

---

[*] Prepared By Vladimir N. Pregelj, Specialist in International Trade and Finance, Economics Division.

Monetary Fund, the world Bank Group, the General Agreement on Tariffs and Trade, or the prospective world Trade Organization, and the Multifiber Arrangement), which to some extent also directly affects bilateral U.S.-North Korean economic relations.

The measures whereby the existing restrictions on U.S.-North Korean economic relations can be removed or mitigated depend primarily on the type of authority under which they have been imposed. Most are mandated by statutes affecting a group of countries (e.g., "Communist," or other similarly described countries) which include North Korea either specifically or by implication. Such statutes may, however, contain an element of executive discretion, generally subject to statutory conditions for its use. Other restrictions have been imposed under general statutory authorities that have been applied to North Korea by executive decision in response to specific situations or policy goals.

Consequently, certain restrictions can be lifted only by the enactment of measures repealing or modifying the applicable statutory mandate, others can be revoked by executive action as authorized by and subject to the conditions, if any, imposed by the relevant statute, and others still might be repealed at executive discretion alone. All restrictions, of course, can be removed by specific legislation.

Measures reducing or removing some restrictions on U.S. commercial transactions with North Korea are expected to be taken in the near term in view of the framework agreement between the two countries on North Korean nuclear issues, reached in Geneva on October 21, 1994 (see p. 10). Under the agreement, "the two sides will move toward full normalization of political and economic relations." Specifically, "within three months of the date of this document, both sides will reduce barriers to trade and investment, including restrictions on telecommunications services and financial transactions."

EMBARGO ON ALL TRANSACTIONS

The most comprehensive U.S. measures restricting economic relations with North Korea is a virtually total and strictly enforced embargo on U.S. trade and financial relations with North Korea. Following the mid-1950 imposition of a ban or exports to North Korea, triggered by North Korea's attack of South Korea (see below: control of U.S. Exports), the comprehensive embargo was imposed under the "national emergency" authority of section 5(b) of the Trading with the Enemy Act (TWEA). The embargo was based on the proclamation of a national emergency (Pres. Proc. 2914; 15 F.R. 9029) after the escalation of the North Korean conflict by the entry of Chinese forces into it.[35] The embargo was implemented as of December 17, 1950 (15 F.R. 9040) through Foreign Assets control Regulations (31 C.F.R. part 500), which are administered and have been modified in various ways by the Office of Foreign Assets Control (OFAC) of the Department of the Treasury.

Although the "national emergency" authorities of the TWEA were repealed in late 1977 and replaced by the International Emergency Economic Powers Act (IEEPA) 50 U.S.C. 1701-1706), the measures taken in exercising the original TWEA national emergency authorities (e.g., the North Korean embargo) have been continued in effect through annual determinations by the President that extensions of such authorities are in the national interest of the United States. The latest such determination extended the North Korean embargo through September 14, 1995 (Presidential Determination No. 94-46, September 8, 1994, 59 F.R. 47229).

The regulatory mechanics of the embargo consists of a general ban on commercial and financial transactions, which can take place only if they are authorized by regulation (general license), or specifically licensed by OFAC. One general license under the Foreign Assets Control Regulations, major in scope, permits exports to North Korea (31 C.F.R. 500.533), provided they have been licensed or otherwise authorized by the Bureau of Export Administration (BXA) in the Department of commerce under the Export Administration Act and related regulations (see below: control of U.S. Exports). With the operational control over exports in the hands of the BXA, the OFAC, in practice, controls only imports from and financial transactions with North Korea, including the blocking of North Korean assets n the United States (amounting to $9.1 million). Regulations also permit certain types of marginal financial transactions, such as limited remittances to individuals in North Korea for necessary living expenses, transactions incidental to individual travel to, in, and from North Korea, and to travel of North Korean individuals to, from, and in the United States, and importation or exportation of informational materials. Specific licenses are issued for imports of small value gifts of North Korean original and, on a case-by-case basis, for travel agencies to provide travel services in connection with travel to North Korea for noncommercial tours or various private exchange programs.

---

[35] Identical embargo, imposed at the same time on China, was lifted in June 1971.

Apart from its possible removal or modification by specific legislation, the embargo on all transactions with North Korea – including the blocking of North Korean assets in the United States – can be removed or modified by executive action. This could take place in several ways: by instituting a policy of approving on a case-by-case basis, instead of denying, the licenses required under current regulations; by changing the restrictiveness of the regulations with respect to North Korea (e.g., by increasing the scope of transactions permitted by various, if still marginal, general licenses); or, definitively, by revoking their applicability to North Korea by striking North Korea from the list of countries subject to Foreign Assets Control Regulations (31 C.F.R. 500.201).[36]

U.S. IMPORTS

In addition to being generally prohibited under the comprehensive embargo, U.S. imports from North Korea are subject to two other separate restrictions, in practice of virtually no consequence while the embargo remains in force and generally of lesser impact: the denial of the nondiscriminatory (most-favored-nation: MFN) status; and ineligibility for the U.S. generalized system of preferences.

Most-Favored-Nation (MFN) Status

Lack of North Korea's MFN status in its trade with the United States means, mainly, that the United States would assess customs duties on imports from North Korea essentially at the high rates enacted by the projectionist Tariff Act of 1930 rather than at the substantially lower rates resulting from concessions granted by the United States in subsequent negotiations with other countries. Because of long-standing U.S. statutory policy, dating back to 1934 and at present stated in section 126 of the Trade Act of 1974 (19 U.S.C. 2136), and, in most cases, also obligations under various international trade agreements, concessional rates granted to any country are applied as a matter of general policy to imports from all U.S. trading partners.

---

[36] In addition to North Korea: Cambodia and, for transactions that took place before February 3, 1994, Vietnam.

This policy was changed by section 5 of the Trade Agreements Extension Act of 1951 (65 Stat. 73), which required the President to suspend MFN status of most Communist countries. The suspension was implemented generally by Presidential Proclamation 2935 of August 1, 1951 (16 F.R. 7635) and specifically for "any part of Korea which may be under communist domination or control" by Trade Agreement Letter of the same date with effect on Sept. 1, 1951 (16 F.R. 7637). This provision remained in the form of a regulation until it was incorporated into the Tariff Schedules of the United States (TSUS), a completely revised and restructured form of the United States basic tariff document, enacted in 1962. In General Headnote 3(e) (later redesignated 3(d)), the TSUS contained a list of "Communist countries" denied MFN status, including "Korea (any part of which may be under communist domination or control)."

This identification was modified somewhat in a new thorough revision of the tariff document (Harmonized Tariff Schedule of the United States – HTS; 19 U.S. 1202; not codified), which was enacted by section 1204 of the Omnibus Trade and competitiveness Act of 1988 (19 U.S.C. 3004) and entered into force on January 1, 1989. Countries denied MFN status, listed in its General Headnote 3(b), including "North Korea," were no longer referred to as "Communist countries" but merely listed as countries the imports from which were subject to "Rate of Duty Column 2" (i.e., the full, non-MFN rate).

Meanwhile, the denial of MFN status to North Korea was reaffirmed by section 401 of the Trade Act of 1974 (19 U.S.C. 2431),[37] which required continued denial of MFN status to any country denied such status at the time of its enactment, except as otherwise provided in Title IV of the Act. The procedure of Title IV, applicable to "nonmarket economy" (NME) countries (of which North Korea is one),[38] requires compliance with the provisions of the freedom-of-emigration (usually referred to as Jackson-Vanik) amendment (sec. 402; 19 U.S.C. 2432), and the conclusion of a bilateral trade agreement and its implementation by enactment (sec. 405; 19 U.S.C. 2435).

The requirements of the Jackson-Vanik amendment can be fulfilled by either (1) a Presidential determination that North Korea is in full compliance with the freedom-of-emigration requirements of the amendment, or (2) a

---

[37] Unless otherwise stated, further references to statutory titles or sections in this part of the report are those to the Trade Act of 1974.
[38] This is the procedure under which MFN status has been extended to and is annually being renewed with respect to most present or former "Communist" countries, including China.

waiver of such compliance by the President if he has determined that such waiver will substantially promote the objectives of the amendment. The determination of full compliance must be renewed semiannually and is subject, at year-end to disapproval by a joint resolution, enacted under a special fast-track procedure (sec. 152; 19 U.S.C. 2192). Waivers of full compliances are issued under the waiver authority originally granted in 1975 and automatically renewable, under specified conditions, every mid-year; annual renewals of the waiver authority also are subject to joint resolutions of disapproval (which may target individual countries), enacted by a fast-track procedure applicable only to such disapprovals (sec. 153; 19 U.S.C. 2193). The initial issuance of a waiver does not require noncongressional approval nor is it subject to congressional disapproval.

The trade agreement required by law must contain a reciprocal grant of MFN status as well as several safeguard provisions. Its implementation must be approved by the enactment of a joint resolution (sec. 407(c)(1); 19 U.S.C. 2437(c)(1)), considered under the same fast-track procedure (sec. 151; 19 U.S.C. 2191) (but without being subject to the additional detailed procedural conditions) as other trade agreements (e.g., the Uruguay Round agreements). By its own terms, such trade agreement remains in force for three-year periods but may be renewed virtually automatically. Such renewals are not subject to congressional approval or disapproval.

Closely tied in with the provisions of section 401 are those of section 409 (19 U.S.C. 2439), which bar the extension of MFN status to an NME country which denies or places serious obstacles to a citizen's right to emigrate to join a close relative in the United States. Affecting the same countries as section 402, this provision does not apply to any country with respect to which a Jackson-Vanik amendment determination or waiver is in effect.

The United States also accords MFN status as a reciprocal obligation under the General Agreement on Tariffs and Trade (GATT) to the parties to the Agreement. In the event that North Korea, which is not now nor has made any moves toward becoming a party to the GATT, were to accede to the GATT—or, rather, to its institutional successor, the world Trade Organization (WTO), once it is established – the United States could avoid its MFN obligation under the GATT or the WTO toward North Korea by invoking, respectively, GATT Article XXXV or WTO Article XIII. Either provision allows reciprocal nonapplication of the GATT or, respectively, the Uruguay Round agreements between a current and a newly acceding party to the GATT or the WTO if either does not consent to it.

Generalized System of Preferences

North Korea also is denied the status of "beneficiary developing country" (BDC) under the U.S. generalized system of preferences (GSP) (secs. 501-505; 19 U.S.C. 2641-2645), which permits a substantial array of products of countries designated as BDCs to be imported into the United States under certain conditions free of duty. North Korea has not been designated a BDC and, consequently, does not appear in the list of designated BDCs contained in General Note 4(a) of the HTS.

Designation of a country as a BDC is subject to a number of conditions several of which would clearly appear to be relevant with respect to North Korea (sec. 502(b); 19 U.S.C. 2462(b)). Designation is denied, for example, generally, to a country that: aids or abets international terrorism;[39] does not afford internationally recognized worker rights to its workers; or, if a Communist country, does not have MFN status with the United States, is not a party to the General Agreement on Tariffs and Trade (GATT) nor a member of the International Monetary Fund (IMF), and is controlled by international communism. While compliance with the antiterrorist and the worker rights conditions may be waived by the President if he determines that the designation of a country as a BDC is in the national economic interest of the United States. The Community-country restriction may not.

As to the conditions applicable solely to Communist countries: North Korea is denied MFN status by the United States and is neither a party to the GATT nor a member of the IMF, but, arguably, could be considered as not being controlled by international communism, an aspect to be definitely determined at the time of the eventual designation.

Once the conditions for designation are fulfilled or, if waivable, waived, a country may be designated as a BDC of the GSP by Presidential action alone and neither requires approval by Congress nor is subject to disapproval by Congress (other than by specific legislation).[40]

CONTROL OF U.S. EXPORTS

The United States has controlled most commercial exports of civilian-use articles to foreign countries, primarily for national security and/or foreign policy reasons, under the authority of a succession of export control

---

[39] For more detail, see below: Control of U.S. Exports.
[40] GSP legislation expired October 1, 1994. Measures to extend it are pending.

acts dating back to 1949 and most recently reenacted as the Export Administration Act of 1979 and since amended several times (50 U.S.C. App. 2401-2420).[41] Just as the scope of the legislation has expanded over the years, so also has the scope and detail of export control regulations, now codified at 15 C.F.R. 769-799.2 as Export Administration Regulations, and promulgated and administered under statutory policies and guidelines by the Bureau of Export Administration (BXA) of the Department of Commerce.

Under present regulations, the scope and severity of controls applicable to exports to any country depends on the country group to which a country is assigned, where the degree of restrictiveness is reflected in the range of articles that require an individual "validated" license for each shipment (or group of related shipments) to a certain destination. The greater the number of articles requiring a validated license, the more restrictive the export control, not only quantitatively but also qualitatively in the sense that validated license may also be denied. Validated licenses are not required for exports that may take place under a general license, that is, a regulation which, in effect, gives an advance blanket permission for a specific type of export. The assignment of countries to their groups and the application of specific licensing requirements are done by the BXA.

The statutory export control authority, specifically the Export Control Act of 1949, was used to impose, on June 28, 1950, as an immediate reaction to North Korea's attack on south Korea, the earliest restriction on U.S. trade with North Korea: an export embargo, by suspending all licenses, general as well as validated, for exports to North Korea (15 F.R. 4189). While this embargo later became part of the comprehensive embargo on all transactions imposed in December 1950 under a different authority, its administration has remained with the export control agency rather than OFAC (see above: Embargo on all Transactions).

After the February 1994 lifting of the embargo on Vietnam, North Korea is one of the only two countries – the other being Cuba – still remaining in Country Group Z (15 C.F.R. Part 770, Supplement No. 1), the group subject to the heaviest restrictions, amounting to a virtually total embargo on exports. The mechanics of the embargo consist of the requirement that, for foreign policy purposes, virtually all exports to group Z countries must be approved by validated licenses, and of the stated general policy to deny all applications for them (15 C.F.R. 785.1).

---

[41] The Act expired in June 1994; its provisions are carried out under Executive Order 12923 of June 30, 1994 (59 FR. 34551), issued under the authority of sec. 101(b) of P.L. 95-223 (Title I – Amendments to the Trading with the Enemy Act) (50 U.S.C. App. 5 note), until the Act itself is extended by legislation.

Altogether excepted from the validated license requirement are informational materials (books, newspapers, journals, movies, maps) (15 C.F.R. 785.1), and gift parcels of limited value, content, and frequency (15 C.F.R. 771.18). While requiring specific approval, "Humanitarian Licenses" are issued, under specified conditions, for exports of donated goods to meet basic human needs (15 C.F.R. 773.5 and Part 773, Supplement No. 7); commercially supplied goods to meet basic human needs, in quantities larger than allowed by the humanitarian license, and exports to meet emergency needs that do not qualify for the humanitarian license are considered on a case-by-case basis (15 C.F.R. 785.1).

In addition to the embargo on exports to North Korea as such, a separate foreign-policy restriction applies to exports to North Korea as a country supporting international terrorism. As provided for in sec. 6(j) of the Export Administration Act of 1979, as amended (50 U.S. C. App. 2405(j))), the Secretary of State, on January 20, 1988, determined "that North Korea is a country which has repeatedly provided support for acts of international terrorism" (53 F.R. 3477). As a consequence of such determination, exports to the country involved of goods or technology that are determined of being able to make a significant contribution to its military potential, or enhance its ability to support acts on international terrorism, require a validated license. Denial of the license, in effect constitutes a ban on such exports. The determination is also cause for sanctions in other economic relations, such as denial of eligibility for the generalized system of preferences, and denial of foreign income tax credit under income tax law (see above: Generalized System of Preferences, and below: Private Foreign Investment).[42]

This regulation may be temporarily suspended or modified in the interest of the security and foreign policy of the United States (22 C.F.R. 126.4), or an exception to it made under specified conditions (22 C.F.R. 126.2) to allow the licensing of exports of Munitions List articles and services to North Korea. The regulation itself can be amended administratively within its statutory intent.

In the case of government-to-government military sales, section 3(a) (1) of the Arms Export Control Act (22 U.S.C. 2753(a)(1)) prohibits the U.S.

---

[42] An identical determination, provided for in sec. 620A of the Foreign Assistance Act of 1961 (22 U.S.C. 2371), cars the affected country (e.g., North Korea) from receiving any assistance under the Foreign Assistance Act, the Agricultural Trade Development and Assistance Act of 1954 ("P.L. 480"), the Peace Corps Act, or the Export-Import Bank Act of 1945 (see below: Bilateral Economic Assistance). In practice, the same determination is made for the purpose of both statutes.

Government from selling or leasing defense articles or services unless the President funds that the furnishing of such articles or services to a country or international organization would strengthen the security of the United States and promote world peace.

In addition to special provisions for controlling exports to any destination of nuclear-related commodities placed on the "nuclear referral list" because of their possible "dual use" (15 C.F.R. 778.2), which are administered by the BXA under the Export Administration Act (see p. 40), a separate control regime is in effect for exports of nuclear equipment and material[43] and is administered by the Nuclear Regulatory Commission in conjunction with the State Department under the authority of the Atomic Energy Act of 1946, as amended. Regulations governing trade in nuclear equipment and material are contained in 10 C.F.R. Part 110, section 110.28 of which lists North Korea as an embargoed destination.

EXPORTS FROM FOREIGN COUNTRIES

Exports from foreign countries to North Korea are to some extent affected by Transaction Control Regulations (31 C.F.R. 505). With some exceptions, these prohibit a U.S. person to engage in any transaction to connection with the sale or purchase in any foreign country, and shipment to any country of the former Sino-Soviet block (or its successors), including North Korea, of any merchandise include din the list of articles at one time subject to international controls of the now defunct Coordinating Committee for multilateral Export Controls (COCOM), or prohibited by U.S. munitions or nuclear control provisions. This prohibition was promulgated on July 23, 1953 (18 F.R. 4291), with respect to all countries of the then Sino-Soviet Bloc and is maintained in force under the same authority and administered in the same way as Foreign Assets Control Regulations (see above: Embargo on all Transactions). While shipments originating in 23 Western countries have been excepted from this prohibition, the exception does not apply to shipments to North Korea. These provisions are administered and can be modified by the Office of Foreign Assets Control.

---

[43] Virtually identical restrictions apply also to imports of nuclear equipment and material.

EXPORT FINANCING

Financing of exports to North Korea through export credits is restricted or affected in several ways. Participation in any U.S. Government program that extends export credits or export credit guarantees or insurance is prohibited to any nonmarket economy country (including North Korea) unless the freedom-of-emigration requirements of the Jackson-Vanik amendment are fulfilled. The principal export-financing programs affected by this restriction are export credits and credit guarantees or insurance of the Export-Import Bank of the United States and the commodity Credit Corporation.

The prohibitions of North Korea's access to U.S. Government export credits and export credit guarantees or insurance contained in the Jackson-Vanik amendment can be removed by the President in either of the two ways provided in that amendment for compliance with its requirements (a determination of full compliance, or a waiver) for the restoration of the MFN status (see above: Most-Favored-nation (MFN) Status). However, although functionally related to it, a country's (North Korea's) access to U.S. Government financial facilities is not contingent on its having been extended MFN status,[44] nor is it subject to congressional approval or disapproval.

The Export-Import Bank of the United States also is specifically prohibited by its own organic law (sec. 2(b)(2)), Export-Import Bank Act of 1945; 12 U.S.C. 635(b)(2)) from engaging in any type of credit transaction (credit, credit guarantee or insurance) for the benefit of any "Marxist-Leninist" country, among them North Korea, unless the President determines *either* (1) that the country has ceased to be a Marxist-Leninist country, *or* (2) that such transactions are in the national interest. A separate determination of national interest is needed for any Eximbank loan of $50 million or more.

North Korea is also barred by sec. 620A of the Foreign Assistance Act of 1961, as amended 922 U.S.C. 2371) from participation in the Eximbank's facilities as a country determined to have provided support to acts of international terrorism, but the restriction is waivable (see below: Bilateral Economic Assistance).

North Korea's access to Eximbank's credit facilities would, consequently, be subject to compliance with, or waiver of, the requirements

---

[44] As a past example: a Jackson-Vanik waiver was issued on December 29, 1990 (E.O. 12740, 56 F.R. 355) for the then still existing Soviet Union, to a substantial extent in order to allow it access to U.S. export credit facilities, but

of the (1) Jackson-Vanik amendment, (2) Marxist-Leninist provision, and (3) counter-terrorist provision, none of which would, however, need to involve congressional actin.

PRIVATE FOREIGN INVESTMENT

American private investment in North Korea falls under the embargo on all transactions with North Korea. Were the embargo to be lifted, such investment would still be adversely affected by three provisions involving the investors' ability to use the facilities of the Overseas Private Investment Corporation (OPIC), a U.S. Government agency insuring or guaranteeing American private investments in developing countries. One is the prohibition, contained in the Jackson-Vanik amendment, of investment guarantees for investments in nonmarket economy countries that do not comply with the requirements of that amendment (see above the implications of the Jackson-Vanik amendment for Eximbank operations); the other two consist of restrictions placed on OPCI operations by virtue of OPIC legislation being part of foreign assistance legislation (see below p. 33-34) in (a) Communist countries and (b) countries determined under scc. 6(j) of the Export Administration Act of 1979 as providing support to acts of international terrorism (see above p. 27).

The terrorist country determination also plays a role in two provisions of the U.S. income tax law, functionally related to American private foreign investments, which create certain disadvantages for incomes originating directly or indirectly in such countries. Section 901(j) of the Internal Revenue Code (26 U.S.C. 901(j)) disallows any credit to U.S. taxpayers for taxes paid or accrued to such countr5yies (as well as those with which the United States does not have diplomatic relations) on income, war profits, or excess profits. Moreover, under section 952(a)(5) of the Code (26 U.S.C. 952(a)(5)), income of any controlled foreign corporation (CFC) a foreign corporation in which U.S. shareholders own 50 percent of the voting power of all voting stock, or 50 percent of total stock value) derived from a country while it is on the terrorist support list is considered "Subpart F income." While U.S. income taxes on foreign-source income of U.S. shareholders of foreign corporations generally may be deferred until the income is actually

---

MFN status was not extended to any part of the by then (in December 1991) dissolved soviet Union until June 9192.

distributed, "Subpart F. income" to a shareholder is taxable when earned by a CFC, whether distributed or not.

EXPANDED ECONOMIC ASSISTANCE AND SUPPORT FOR NORTH KOREA: WHAT STEPS COULD THE UNITED STATES TAKE?[*]

With the end of economic support from the Soviet Union and the continuation of systemic problems associated with a highly centrally planned economy, economic conditions in North Korea have declined dramatically in recent years. The North Korean economy contracted by a reported 20 percent between 1989 and 1993, with output declining by an estimated 10-15 percent in 1992 alone .The country suffers from chronic food shortages that have led to short-term austerity measures but no long-term solutions to the food security problem. If the recently signed nuclear agreement proceeds successfully and North Korea becomes a less isolated nation, it might be expected that Pyongyang will seek external economic assistance from bilateral aid donors like the United States, and membership in the International Monetary Fund (IMF), the World Bank, and the Asian Development Bank.

The United States has never extended any type of foreign assistance to North Korea and numerous legislative restrictions stand in the way of future consideration of economic aid initiatives. These same legal impediments would also block the use of foreign aid resources to finance the procurement of heavy oil for North Korea that the U.S. pledged as part of the nuclear agreement between the two countries. Restrictions also exist governing U.S. actions in the international financial institutions that would impede North Korean membership and access to the facilities of these multilateral organizations.

BILATERAL ECONOMIC ASSISTANCE[45]

Although several restrictions stand in the way of he initiation of a regular U.S. bilateral foreign aid program, the most explicit prohibition – and one that does not include a direct Presidential waiver authority – appears as section 507 of the Foreign Operations Appropriations Act, FY 1995 (P.L. 103-306). Section 507 prohibits any assistance provided under the Act for direct (bilateral) aid to a list of countries, including North Korea. Though Congress has included a list of prohibited countries in annual foreign aid appropriation measures dating back to 1974, North Korea was added for the first time in the FY 1995 act.[46]

If the Administration wanted to use foreign aid funds for North Korea, it would have to pursue one of two routes: convince Congress to drop North Korea from this list in next year's Foreign Operations Appropriations bill, something that would not lift the ban on using FY 1995 funds for financing the oil or launching other programs; or the President could utilize his special and most expansive foreign policy waiver authority, found in section 614(a) of the Foreign Assistance Act of 1961, to lift the immediate prohibition of section 507. Section 614(a) allows the President to provide assistance (up to

---

[*] Prepared by Larry Q. Nowels, Specialist in Foreign Affairs, Foreign Affairs and National Defense Division.

[45] Bilateral economic assistance primarily involves programs administered by the U.S. Agency for International Development, but may also include aid activities including those of the Overseas Private Investment Corporation, the Trade and Development Agency, the Peace Corps, the State Department's narcotics control program, and others depending on the scope of the legislative restrictions noted below.

[46] North Korea was added to the ineligible country list during the House-Senate Conference Committee on the Foreign Operations appropriation bill in early August 1994. The House-passed measure contained no references to the DPRK while the Senate version of H.R. 4426 included an amendment banning funds in that or any other act for North Korea unless the President certified that the DPRK did not possess nuclear weapons, had halted its nuclear program, and had not exported weapons, had halted its nuclear program, and had not exported weapons-grade plutonium. Sponsors of the Senate amendment expressed concern over what they regarded as a series of concessions made by U.S. negotiators during talks with North Korea over the past 18 months. They saw foreign aid as an additional "carrot" that American officials might use in subsequent discussions, and wanted to ensure that U.S. assistance would not be offered unless the DPRK took significant steps to terminate its nuclear program. Conferees deleted the Senate amendment, which would have blocked the use of any U.S. funds for assisting North Korea, but added the DPRK to the section 507 list of countries prohibited from receiving Foreign Operation funds.

$50 million annually per country) to a nation otherwise prohibited by determining that o do so is important to the security interests of the United States, and notifies Congress in writing. Because of the far-reaching nature of the section 614(a) authority, the President is required to consult with, and provide a written policy justification to the House Foreign Affairs Committee, the Senate Foreign Relations Committee, and the House and Senate Foreign Operations Appropriations Subcommittees. In practice, past Presidents have used the authority sparingly and with close consultation with Congress.

While the removal of North Korea from the list of section 507 countries would eliminate the most direct aid prohibition, several other foreign assistance laws or ban or potentially block assistance to North Korea. Each, however, contains a waiver authority that the President would presumably exercise if he chose to use the section 614(a) waiver. Provisions applying to North Korea include:

- **Communist country prohibition** – section 620(f) of the Foreign Assistance Act of 1961 (FAAct, 61) prohibits U.S. aid to Communist countries. North Korea is on the list of Communist countries included in section 620(f). The President may exempt a country from this restriction if he determines and reports to Congress that to do so would be important to the national interest of the United States.

- **Terrorist country prohibition** – section 620A of the FAAct, 61, bans assistance under that Act, food aid under P.L. 480, Peace Corps assistance, or Export-Import Bank credit facilities for countries that the Secretary of State has determined to have repeatedly supported acts of international terrorism. The Secretary designated North Korea as a terrorist country on January 20, 1988.[47] The President can *waive* this prohibition after consulting with Congress and determining that national security interests or humanitarian reasons warrant the resumption of assistance. The president may also *remove* a country

---

[47] The Secretary designated North Korea as a terrorist country under the authority of section 6(j) of the Export Administration Act of 1979, and not under the authority of section 620A.

from the list of terrorist nations, if he certifies to Congress that either, (1) thee has been a fundamental change in leadership and government policies, the government is no longer supporting acts of terrorism and it has provided assurances that it will not to do so in the future, or (2) 45 days in advance of removing the terrorist designation, the government has not supported acts of terrorism for the past six months and has provided assurance that it will not do so in the future. Congress has included a similar prohibition and waiver authority annually since FY 1988 in the Foreign Operations Appropriations Act (at present section 529 of the FY 1995 appropriation, P.L. 103-306).

- **Non-nuclear weapons state prohibition** – section 530(b) of the Foreign Relations Authorization Act, FY 1994-95 (P.L. 103-236), prohibits any assistance under the FAAct, 61, to any non-nuclear weapon state that the President has found to have "terminated, abrogated, or materially violated" an International Atomic Energy Agency (IAEA) safeguards agreement or violated a bilateral U.S. nuclear cooperation agreement. The IAEA has found North Korea to have violated its safeguards agreement. The President may waive this prohibition if he reports to Congress in advance that the prohibition of aid would be "seriously prejudicial" to the achievement of U.S. nonproliferation goals or would "jeopardize the common defense and security."

One additional restriction concerning human rights violations might also potentially apply, although no determination has been made. Sections 116 (development aid) and 502B (security aid) for the FAAct, 61, ban assistance to the governments of countries that consistently violate the human rights of its people.

Despite these broad restrictions limiting possible U.S. economic assistance to North Korea, a few programs administered by the Agency for International Development (USAID) are exempt from any legislative prohibitions. Presumably, the President could extend these activities – for child survival programs and for research on and treatment and control of AIDS – to the DPRK without issuing any waivers. USAID can also provide foreign disaster relief in any country regardless of aid prohibitions that would otherwise prohibit U.S. assistance.

FOOD ASSISTANCE

The Agricultural Trade Development and Assistance Act of 1954 ("PL 480") (P.L. 83-480) authorizes the transfer, on both a grant and credit basis, of U.S. agricultural commodities to developing and least developed countries facing foreign exchange shortages, difficulties in purchasing food needs through commercial channels, food deficits and high levels of malnutrition, and emergency food requirements. So long as North Korea meets these requirements, presumably, it could be declared eligible for U.S. food assistance. (As noted above, however, the President would first have to waive section 620A of the FAAct, 61, or remove North Korea from the list of terrorist states.) Regardless of these general eligibility requirements, emergency food aid under title II of PL 480 may be extended notwithstanding any other limitation or prohibition. Congress repealed in 1990 a general exclusion for Communist countries which the President would have had to waive for the DPRK if it were still in force.

MULTILATERAL ECONOMIC ASSISTANCE

North Korea is not a member of the International Monetary Fund (IMF), the World Bank or the Asian Development Bank, so that existing restrictions on U.S. contributions to these institutions and lending to countries like North Korea would not apply at the present time. Should the DPRK seek membership in the future, the United States could take steps to facilitate North Korean admittance or to oppose it.[48] Once a member, however,

---

[48] To become a member of these institutions, country applications must be approved by a majority vote of the Boards of Governors. Generally, eligibility is based on the country's willingness to meet economic standards that apply to all members. The IMF, for example requires that members avoid restrictive foreign exchange practices and all institutions insist on receipt of information concerning internal economic affairs of their members. The United States would have a voice in the decision-making process, but could not unilaterally veto North Korea's application.

several legislative restrictions, unless waived, would require U.S. executive directors to these institutions to oppose loans for the DPRK:

- **Selected countries prohibited from indirect assistance** – beginning with the FY 1992 Foreign Operations Administrations, Congress annually has included North Korea in a list of countries that are ineligible from receiving assistance "indirectly" – that is, through multilateral organizations – from the United States. The President may waive this restriction, as he has done annually, if he certifies that it is in the U.S. national interest. (The current prohibition is in section 523 of the Foreign Operations Appropriations, FY 1995.)

- **Communist dictatorships** -- section 43 of the Bretton Woods Agreements Act (22 U.S.C. 286aa) – commonly referred to as the "Gramm Amendment" – requires the Secretary of the Treasury to instruct the U.S. Executive Director of the IMF to "actively oppose" the use of any IMF credit facility by a "Communist dictatorship" (not further defined, but presumably including North Korea) unless the Secretary of the Treasury, upon request, at least 21 days before the IMV vote on approving such use, certifies that the loan meets a series of economic criteria.

- **Terrorist nations** – section 528 of the FY 1995 Foreign Operations Appropriations requires the Secretary of the Treasury to instruct each U.S. Executive Director to international financial institutions (IFIs) to oppose any loan to a country that the Secretary of State has designated (under section 6(j) of the Export Administration Act of 1979) as a terrorist state. As noted above, the Secretary determined on January 20, 1988 that North Korea repeatedly supported international acts of terrorism.

- **Non-nuclear weapon state** -- section 823 of the Foreign Relations Authorization Act, FY 1994-95, requires the Secretary of the Treasury to instruct U.S. IFI Executive Directors to oppose use of the institutions' funds "to promote the acquisition of unsafeguarded special nuclear material or the development, stockpiling, or use of nuclear explosive device by any non-nuclear weapon state."

As with restrictions concerning bilateral assistance, requirements to oppose IFI loans based on human rights conditions might also apply if a determination applicable to North Korea was made (section 7001 of the International Financial Institutions Act).

Present U.S. law also affects potentially U.S. contributions to international organizations, such as the UN Development Program, that assist North Korea. Section 516 of the Foreign Operations Appropriations Act, 1995, states that, at the discretion of the President, the United States may withhold a share of its voluntary contribution to various UN and other international organizations in proportion to the amount of aid such organizations might have provided to Communist countries listed under section 620(f) of the Foreign Assistance Act of 1961.

NUCLEAR COOPERATION AND NONPROLIFERATION[*]

On August 12, 1994, the United States and North Korea announced an agreement in principle to exchange North Korea's current nuclear program for new reactors that would be less suited for nuclear weapons. The State Department proposal would assist North Korea in acquiring two light water reactors (LWRs) in exchange for a "freeze" on its current nuclear program. The "freeze" would require an end to construction at the Yongbyon reprocessing facility and at two reactors that are nearing completion, and their eventual dismantlement. An international consortium – the Korea Energy Development Organization – would facilitate the transfer of replacement reactors. The delivery of the reactors is to take place over a ten-year period if North Korea complies with its obligations under the Non-Proliferation Treaty (NPT) and its safeguards agreement with the International Atomic Energy Agency (IAEA).[49] Negotiations during September and October produced a framework agreement which was

---

[*] Prepared by Zachary S. Davis, Analyst in International Nuclear Policy, Environment and Natural Resources Division.

[49] South Korea and the United States have agreed that South Korea should build the reactors. Seoul has agreed to pay about 60-75 percent of the estimated cost of around $4 billion, with Japan and perhaps other countries contributing the rest of the money. The deal would also provide "interim energy alternatives" to North Korea until the new reactors begin operation. North Korea at one point rejected this offer, apparently because it would rather have Russian or German reactors as well as $2 billion in compensation. "Agreed Statement of August 12th, 1994"; State Department Briefing, September 21, 1994; R.Jeffrey Smith, "Demands by North Korea Puzzle U.S. Negotiators," *Washington Post*, September 23, 1994, A32.

announced by President Clinton on October 18 and signed by the United States and North Korea on October 21.[50]

This section focuses o the parameters that would permit U.S. nuclear cooperation with North Korea, including participation in the proposed reactor transfer. Some questions remain about the precise nature and timing of the U.S. role in the reactor transfer. The requirements for direct U.S. nuclear cooperation may not apply for the near term, but could be relevant at a later stage in the reactor construction project if the U.S., U.S. companies, or U.S. allies are to make material contributions to North Korea's nuclear program.[51] Other restrictions could apply depending on the terms of the transfer.

STATUTORY REQUIREMENTS FOR NUCLEAR COOPERATION

Two laws govern direct nuclear cooperation between the U.S. and a foreign country: the Atomic Energy Act of 1954 (P.L. 83-703) and the Nuclear Nonproliferation Act of 1978 (P.L. 95-242).[52] These laws establish criteria that must be satisfied as a condition for nuclear cooperation.

Foremost among the criteria is the requirement that a bilateral agreement for nuclear cooperation be in force between the U.S. and a foreign government.[53]

Other criteria in the Atomic Energy Act (AEA), as amended by the (NNPA) could restrict U.S. nuclear exports to North Korea. Section 123(a)(2) of the AEA (42 U.S.C. 2153(a)(2)) requires that "IAEA safeguards be maintained with respect to all nuclear materials in all peaceful nuclear activities within the territory" of any non-nuclear weapon state as a condition

---

[50] Statement by President Bill Clinton regarding U.S.-North Korea Framework Agreement, The White House, October 18, 1994; Special Briefing on U.S.-North Korean Relations, Robert Gallucci, Assistant Secretary of State for Politico-Military Affairs and Ambassador at Large, The White House, October 18, 1994.

[51] The issue of U.S. allies could be relevant in connection with the retransfer of U.S.-origin technology to North Korea.

[52] The Nuclear Nonproliferation Act of 1978 tightened the restrictions on nuclear exports in the Atomic Energy Act of 1954.

[53] Agreements for cooperation are negotiated by the State Department, then reviewed by the Department of Energy, the Nuclear Regulatory Commission, the Arms

for U.S. supply of nuclear technology. The unresolved issue of North Korea's plutonium inventory could present a problem for meeting this requirement. The President may exempt a proposed agreement from the requirements of Section 123 "if he determines that inclusion of any such requirement would be seriously prejudicial to the achievement of United States non-proliferation objectives or otherwise jeopardize to common defense and security."

Export licensing requirements for nuclear technology are contained in Sections 126, 127, and 128 of AEA, as amended by the NNPA (42 U.S.C. 2155, 2156 and 2157). The Nuclear Regulatory Commission (NRC) issues such licenses after consultations with the Departments of State, Energy, Defense, Commerce and the Arms Control and Disarmament Agency . The criteria in sections 126, 127, and 128 include: IAEA safeguards on the export; no use of the export for nuclear weapons; adequate physical security; no retransfer without prior U.S. consent; and no reprocessing of U.S.-origin materials without prior consent. Like section 123 discussed above, section 128 requires full-scope safeguards on all nuclear activities in any non-nuclear weapons state as a condition of export. The President can waive the criteria and authorize an export license that does not satisfy sections 126, 127, and 128, provided that the license is submitted to Congress and Congress does not adopt a concurrent resolution of disapproval (AEA, section 128(b)(1)).

If a nuclear cooperation agreement between the United States and North Korea enters into force, the AEA, as amended, conditions cooperation on compliance with the terms of the agreement. Section 129 on "Conduct Resulting in Termination of Nuclear Exports" (42 U.S.C. 2158) states: "No nuclear materials and equipment or sensitive nuclear technology shall be exported to (1) any non-nuclear weapon state that is found by the President to have, at any time after the effective date of this section:

(A) detonated a nuclear explosive device; or
(B) terminated or abrogated IAEA safeguards;
(C) materially violated an IAEA safeguards; or
(D) engaged in activities involving source or special nuclear material and having direct significant for the manufacture or acquisition of nuclear explosive devices, and has failed to take steps which, in the

---

Control and Disarmament Agency and the President before being sent to Congress.

President's judgment, represent sufficient progress toward terminating such activities.

Points B, C, and D could be relevant in the case of North Korea, depending on the nature of the cooperation.[54]

DUAL-USE TECHNOLOGY

Section 309(c) of the NNPA directs the Department of Commerce to control exports of dual-use equipment that could have nuclear applications. Under the authority of the Export Administration Act of 1979, as amended, the Bureau of Export Administration maintains a Commodity Control List (CCL) as well as a list of controlled countries. The items on the CCL that are subject to nuclear nonproliferation control are known as the Nuclear Referral List.[55] North Korea is a controlled country with respect to nuclear technology. Thus, North Korea's status as a controlled country could bar the United Sates from contributing controlled items to a reactor project in North Korea unless North Korea were removed from the controlled country list, and/or the Commerce Department issued licenses for export of dual-use items to North Korea. However, it may be possible for the United States to provide uncontrolled items such as safety equipment for the storage of spent fuel rods or non-nuclear power generating equipment if such assistance is not barred by other laws.

NUCLEAR-RELATED ASSISTANCE

Several other laws could also restrict U.S. nuclear-related cooperation with North Korea. These mainly affect the non-nuclear aspects of the agreement. In addition to the prohibitions cited above in the Foreign Operations Appropriation FY 1995 and the Foreign Assistance Act of 1961, the Foreign Relations Authorization Act for FY 1994-95, section 530, prohibits U.S. assistance under the 1961 foreign aid act to any non-nuclear

---

[54] The President can waive the restrictions.
[55] The Export Administration Act expired in June 1994 after the 103rd Congress failed to pass new export control legislation. Authority for maintaining export controls is provided by the International Emergency Economic Powers Act (P.L. 95-223.) (se also above: Control of U.S. Exports.)

state *found by the President* to have terminated, abrogated, or materially violated an IAEA safeguards agreement. The IAEA has found North Korea to have violated its safeguards agreement. This restriction, as well as others, could especially narrow U.S. options to provide alternative energy supplies such as oil and/or compensation to North Korea for stopping its current nuclear program.

FINANCIAL ASPECTS OF NUCLEAR COOPERATION

Financing for the reactor construction project is to be arranged through an international consortium. Although it is not clear how or if the United States might contribute materially to the proposed multilateral consortium, U.S. law could restrict certain types of contributions. Most importantly, Congress would have to authorize and appropriate funds for any U.S. financial contribution. Moreover, as mentioned above, several legal impediments stand in the way of utilizing foreign assistance funds for these purposes, although the President maintains waiver authorities.

Regarding international funding, the Foreign Relations Authorization Act for FY 94-95, section 823, amended the International Financial Institutions Act for FY 94-95, section 823, amended the International Financial Institutions Act (22 U.S.C. 262d(a)) to direct the Secretary of the Treasury to instruct U.S. representatives to international financial institutions to oppose the use of the institution's to promote the acquisition of unsafeguarded special nuclear material or the development, stockpiling, or use of any nuclear explosive device by any non-nuclear weapon state. Ongoing problems with undeclared, and therefore unsafeguarded, nuclear materials in North Korea could trigger this restriction with respect to financial institutions such as World Bank, the International Monetary Fund, and the Asian Development Bank. Also, North Korea is not a member of these institutions.

INDEX

A

Agreed Framework, 22, 29, 30, 31, 33, 34, 46, 47, 48, 51, 52
Agricultural Trade Development and Assistance Act, 73, 83
ASEAN Regional Forum, 17
austerity measures, 79

B

Berlin Declaration, 5
Bureau of Export Administration, 67, 72, 90
Bureau of Export Administration (BXA), 67, 72, 74, 90
Bush Administration, 29, 62

C

Carter Administration, 40, 61, 62
Cheju Island, 7
China, 8, 9, 11, 15, 24, 25, 29, 33, 36, 40, 55, 56, 57, 60, 61, 62, 67, 69
Chun Doo Hwan, 41
Clinton Administration, 5, 14, 21, 22, 24, 25, 29, 30, 32, 33, 34, 35, 44, 55, 59, 61
Combined Forces Command, 60, 62
Combined Forces Command (CFC), 60, 61, 62, 76
Commercial Relations, v, 65
Congress, iv, 34, 35, 36, 39, 47, 52, 53, 54, 59, 61, 62, 71, 80, 81, 82, 83, 84, 89, 90, 91

D

Demilitarized Zone, 6
Demilitarized Zone (DMZ), 6, 7, 8, 9, 10, 38

E

economic sanctions, 5, 15, 26, 30, 34
European Union, 32, 33

F

food aid, 6, 7, 9, 16, 24, 81, 83
food assistance, 83
food shortages, 79
Ford Administration, 60
Foreign Assets Control Regulations, 67, 68, 74
Foreign Operations Appropriations Act, 80, 82, 85

Four Party talks, 9

G

General Agreement on Tariffs and Trade, 66, 70, 71
General Agreement on Tariffs and Trade (GATT), 66, 70, 71
Geneva, 37, 39, 44, 45, 46, 48, 66
Grand National Party (GNP), 2, 3

H

human rights, 40, 43, 82, 85
Hyundai, 2, 6

I

International Atomic Energy Agency (IAEA), 21, 23, 27, 29, 30, 31, 42, 44, 45, 46, 49, 51, 82, 87, 88, 89, 91
International Monetary Fund, 66, 71, 79, 83, 91

J

Japan, 3, 8, 13, 14, 15, 16, 17, 18, 19, 20, 22, 25, 26, 28, 31, 32, 47, 87
Jo Myong Rok, 8
Joint Declaration on the Denuclearization of the Korean Peninsula, 44, 46

K

Kim Dae Jung, 1, 2, 3, 5, 15
Kim Il Sung, 40, 45
Korean Peninsula Energy Development Organization (KEDO), 15, 31
Korean War, 2, 34, 36, 37, 38, 39, 42, 59, 62

L

liaison offices, 5, 34, 55
light water reactors, 31, 32, 33, 44, 45, 47, 87
light water reactors (LWRs), 31, 32, 33, 44, 45, 46, 47, 87

M

military relations, 59
missile talks, 8
missile testing, 34
most-favored nation (MFN), 68, 69, 70, 71, 75, 76
Mutual Defense Treaty, 39, 59, 61, 62

N

National Assembly, 3, 19
Nodong missiles, 25
normalization, 8, 13, 14, 16, 17, 18, 19, 34, 35, 36, 37, 45, 50, 54, 66
normalization talks, 8, 13, 14, 17, 19
Northern Limitation Line, 10
Nuclear Non-Proliferation Treaty (NPT), 21, 29, 31, 42, 43, 44, 46, 51, 87
Nuclear Regulatory Commission, 74, 88, 89
nuclear weapons, 14, 16, 21, 22, 23, 24, 26, 27, 28, 29, 30, 31, 32, 43, 44, 45, 50, 80, 87, 89
nuclear-related cooperation, 90

O

Office of Foreign Assets Control, 56, 67, 74
Office of Foreign Assets Control (OFAC), 56, 67, 72, 74
oil, 21, 22, 33, 35, 36, 46, 49, 79, 80, 91

P

Panmunjon, 5, 6, 38, 40, 60
private investment in North Korea, 76
Putin, 15, 26
Pyongyang, 1, 2, 3, 5, 6, 7, 10, 11, 13, 14, 15, 16, 17, 22, 29, 31, 37, 39, 40, 41, 42, 43, 44, 47, 52, 53, 60, 79

R

Reagan Administration, 41
Red Cross, 6, 7, 9
reunification, 1, 15, 41
ROK Defense White Paper, 10
Russia, 27, 28, 33

S

Seoul, 1, 2, 3, 5, 6, 7, 9, 10, 13, 14, 18, 38, 40, 41, 42, 87
Soviet Union, 15, 24, 25, 37, 38, 39, 40, 75, 79
State Department, 18, 26, 27, 28, 55, 56, 74, 80, 87, 88
Status of Forces Agreement, 59, 63
Sunshine Policy, 2, 14

Syngman Rhee, 18

T

Tariff Schedules of the United States, 69
terrorism, 8, 41, 43, 71, 73, 75, 76, 81, 84
Trading with the Enemy Act (TWEA), 42, 66, 67, 72
Treaty of Basic Relations, 18
2+2 peace treaty initiative, 8

U

U.S.-North Korean Agreed Framework, 22
UN Security Council, 60
unification, 5, 11, 19, 39
United Nations Command, 8, 9, 60
United Nations Command (UNC), 8, 9, 38, 40, 60

W

Washington, 8, 22, 24, 28, 37, 39, 41, 44, 52, 55, 62, 87